:HILD DEVELOPMENT

William Damon, *Brown University*
EDITOR-IN-CHIEF

Children's Perspectives on the Family

Inge Bretherton
University of Wisconsin–Madison

Malcolm W. Watson
Brandeis University

EDITORS

Number 48, Summer 1990

JOSSEY-BASS INC., PUBLISHERS
San Francisco • Oxford

Children's Perspectives on the Family.
Inge Bretherton, Malcolm W. Watson (eds.).
New Directions for Child Development, no. 48.

NEW DIRECTIONS FOR CHILD DEVELOPMENT
William Damon, Editor-in-Chief

Microfilm copies of issues and articles are available in 16mm and
35mm, as well as microfiche in 105mm, through University Microfilms
Inc., 300 North Zeeb Road, Ann Arbor, Michigan 48106.

NEW DIRECTIONS FOR CHILD DEVELOPMENT is part of The Jossey-Bass
Social and Behavioral Science Series and is published quarterly by
Jossey-Bass Inc., Publishers (publication number USPS 494-090).
Second-class postage paid at San Francisco, California, and at
additional mailing offices. Postmaster: Send address changes to
Jossey-Bass Inc., Publishers, 350 Sansome Street, San Francisco,
California 94104.

EDITORIAL CORRESPONDENCE should be sent to the Editor-in-Chief,
William Damon, Department of Education, Box 1938, Brown
University, Providence, Rhode Island 02912.

Library of Congress Catalog Card Number LC 85-644581

International Standard Serial Number ISSN 0195-2269

International Standard Book Number ISBN 1-55542-825-8

Cover photograph by Wernher Krutein/PHOTOVAULT, copyright © 1990.
Manufactured in the United States of America. Printed on acid-free paper.

Contents

Editors' Notes

In recent years, investigators have increasingly emphasized the importance of the family as a context for development. Among the many topics that have been explored are the effects of paternal involvement on the mother-child relationship (Parke and Tinsley, 1987), the links between marital satisfaction and the child's socioemotional development (for example, Belsky, Rovine, and Fish, in press; Howes and Markman, 1989), and the development of sibling interactions (Dunn and Kendrick, 1982). At the same time, there have been exciting new findings regarding the development of children's social understanding of self and other (for example, Dunn, 1988; Astington, Harris, and Olson, 1988). So far, however, researchers have not integrated these two broad domains of study in order to examine how children perceive the family.

The main objective of this volume is to bring these two domains together for the first time. Note that our focus is not on the "veridical" family as seen by an outside observer but rather on the child's subjective perceptions and representations. We are putting the child on center stage as a creator of representations rather than as a target of family influences. It is our hope that as we learn more about children's changing perspectives on the family, we will find a common developmental sequence within which qualitative individual differences in the content of these representations can be interpreted and related to children's actual coping with family crises such as separation, Oedipal conflicts, and changes in family configuration.

Each chapter covers some facet of how children from three to twelve years of age represent the family in general and/or their families in particular. In all of the studies, the children are presented with hypothetical situations, whether through questions, pictures, or story stems that are acted out with family dolls. Approaches used for accessing children's representations about family relationships range from direct inquiries about the child's own family (with the aid of supporting props) to more projective assessments via fantasy play with a bear family. In each study, representational assessments of family relationships are validated with other measures, such as observed family or parent-child interactions.

In Chapter One, Molly Reid, Sharon Landesman Ramey, and Margaret Burchinal report on three dialogues designed to systematically probe children's perceptions of themselves and other family members. The instruments are based on Vygotsky's (1978) principles, that is, the children were allowed to collaborate on interactive dialogues that involved the manipulation of personalized props in order to sustain attention, interest, and comprehension. Each of the assessments also had an adult counterpart, so that corresponding child and parent data could be compared. The three dialogue assessments were (1) "What I'm Like and What Others in My Family are Like," (2) "My Family and Friends," and (3) "What Is Important in My Family."

To evaluate these new dialogue techniques, several hundred six- to twelve-year-old children from different ethnic backgrounds and family constellations were studied. Age, sex, and family differences in the children's responses to the dialogues support and augment findings derived from complementary sources (parental reports, behavioral observations). The authors conclude with a discussion of the contribution that children's reports about the family can make to research on the family.

In Chapter Two, Malcolm W. Watson and Kenneth Getz investigate intriguing increases and decreases in so-called Oedipal behaviors and attitudes, that is, preference for the opposite-sex parent and antagonism toward the same-sex parent, in three- to six-year-olds. The authors used two assessment techniques: (1) parents kept diary records of their children's behavior and (2) children enacted doll-play narratives about family conflicts. To complement this information, children's understanding of family roles and of age relativity were evaluated independently. Watson and Getz discovered that Oepidal behaviors increased at four years of age and then declined at five years in synchrony with the cognitive assessment of children's understanding of family role relations.

In Chapter Three, Edward Mueller and Elizabeth Tingley argue that fantasy play, given its freedom and nonanxious quality, allows children to freely reveal representations of self and family members without awareness that they are engaging in indirect self-disclosure. A series of story beginnings involving a bear family was developed in which the child was presented with the same-sex bear child as "your bear." The child was then invited to complete the scenario with the question "What happens next?" The "Bears' Picnic" was administered to thirty four-year-old children from the Harvard Individual Differences Project who had been studied since they were fourteen months old. At twenty months of age, the quality of the mother-child relationship had been examined. Children whose mothers were rated low on sensitivity at twenty months were more likely, at four years, to tell stories that devalued both themselves and their families. The chapter concludes with a thought-provoking discussion of clinical and interpretive issues relevant to the use of play techniques for assessing children's representations.

In Chapter Four, Nancy M. Slough and Mark T. Greenberg describe five-year-olds' responses to pictures of separation from parents, using a modified version of the Klagsbrun-Bowlby Separation Anxiety Test. Bowlby (1973) had hypothesized that in the course of transactions with caregivers and other family members, children develop internal working models of self and other in relationships, working models that play a guiding role in how the children interpret and set out to influence their worlds.

Slough and Greenberg explore children's internal working models of self in relation to parents through a semi-projective test. The test is based on pictures of mild and severe separations from parents. On being shown each picture, the five-year-olds were first asked how the child in the picture feels, what she or he is going to do, and then how they themselves would feel and act under the same circumstances. Children's responses to the pictures were rated on quality of represented attachment, self-reliance, avoidance, and emotional openness. These ratings, done separately for self and pictured child, turned out to be correlated with observed attachment status during a brief laboratory separation-reunion procedure. It was especially interesting that children's representations of their *own* thoughts and feelings about the separation pictures were more highly related to observed attachment quality than their statements about the pictured child. However, children who gave similar responses for self and other child tended to be classified as very securely attached. The authors conclude by pointing out the importance of defensive processes in evaluation of children's perceptions of the family.

In Chapter Five, Inge Bretherton, Charlynn Prentiss, and Doreen Ridgeway examine children's family story completions longitudinally. A prior study by Bretherton and her colleagues had shown that the content and structure of three-year-olds' attachment story completions were related to a variety of other attachment measures at earlier ages and at the same age. The story issues enacted with small, family figures and props ranged from "parent as authority and attachment figure," to a pain and fear situation, to a separation and reunion.

In this chapter the authors reexamine data from the same children longitudinally, with specific emphasis on the changing complexity of family representations between three and four-and-a-half years of age. Even at three years of age most children were able to enact plausible resolutions to the story issues, but at the earlier age the resolutions tended to be closely linked to the story stems as performed by the tester. At four-and-a-half years, resolutions incorporated a larger number of family participants (that is, father, siblings, and, in some of the stories, a grandmother) who were portrayed in much more differentiated roles. The children also demonstrated a budding understanding that family members can occupy multiple roles.

Together, these chapters provide new directions for the field of child development toward the assessment of family systems.

Inge Bretherton
Malcolm W. Watson
Editors

References

Astington, J. W., Harris, P. L., and Olson, D. R. *Developing Theories of Mind.* New York: Cambridge University Press, 1988.

Belsky, J., Rovine, M., and Fish, M. "The Developing Family System." In M. Gunnar (ed.), *Systems and Development: Minnesota Symposium on Child Psychology.* Vol. 22. Hillsdale, N.J.: Erlbaum, in press.

Bowlby, J. *Attachment and Loss.* Vol. 2: *Separation.* New York: Basic Books, 1973.

Dunn, J. *The Beginnings of Social Understanding.* Cambridge, Mass.: Harvard University Press, 1988.

Dunn, J., and Kendrick, C. *Siblings: Love, Envy and Understanding.* Cambridge, Mass.: Harvard University Press, 1982.

Howes, P., and Markman, H. J. "Marital Quality and Child Functioning: A Longitudinal Investigation." *Child Development,* 1989, *60,* 1015–1024.

Parke, R. D., and Tinsley, B. J. "Family Interaction in Infancy." In J. D. Osofsky (ed.), *Handbook of Infant Development.* New York: Wiley, 1987.

Vygotsky, L. S. *Mind in Society: The Development of Higher Psychological Processes.* Cambridge, Mass.: Harvard University Press, 1978.

Inge Bretherton is professor of child and family studies at the University of Wisconsin–Madison.

Malcolm W. Watson is associate professor of psychology at Brandeis University.

*Developmentally sensitive child dialogues reveal that children's
own self-appraisals are linked to their perceptions of their
parents' strengths and weaknesses and to the support they
report receiving from significant others in their lives.*

Dialogues with Children About Their Families

*Molly Reid, Sharon Landesman Ramey,
Margaret Burchinal*

In this chapter, we describe a dialogue technology for probing young
children's perceptions of their families and themselves. First, we posit
that both subjective and objective data are critical to the study of family
functioning, and that the perceptions of all family members can provide
insights into family processes. A conceptual model for viewing family
functioning and the contribution of children's perceptions is presented
in this section. Second, we describe a set of new instruments, Dialogues
About Families, designed to tap children's perceptions about themselves
and their families. The dialogues concern (1) children's attributions
about behavioral qualities in themselves and other family members, (2)
their perceptions of and satisfaction with different types of social support,
and (3) their understanding of family goals and values and their perceptions of different family members' priorities. Because there have been no

This research was supported by the National Institute of Child Health and
Human Development (HD-19348 and HD-24116) and the John D. and Catherine T.
MacArthur Foundation Network on Childhood Transitions. We appreciate the
support services provided by the Child Development and Mental Retardation
Center (HD-02274) and the Frank Porter Graham Child Development Center
(HD-03110). We especially thank TV Kenly for assisting with tables and manu-
script preparation and Janice Rabkin for coordinating data collection. Jim Jac-
card was our colleague in the overall conceptualization and conduct of the Seattle
Family Behavior Study and provided valuable assistance in the instrument development phase. We thank Inge Bretherton, Mick Watson, Irwin Sarason, Barbara
Sarason, Craig Ramey, and Mike Guralnick for their valuable comments.

methods previously available to study all family members throughout the developmental span of early childhood through adulthood, assessment of the reliability and validity of data from a new methodology is critical. Third, we selectively highlight developmental patterns in how children actually perceive their families. We focus on the interdependencies in family members' satisfaction with social support, their attributions about behavioral qualities in one another, and their own self-concepts. Generally, older children evaluate their parents in a more differentiated and less positive manner than do younger children. Somewhat surprising, however, is the finding that despite the increasing importance of peers in children's lives in later middle childhood, their reliance on and satisfaction with parents does not decline. Most importantly, children's perceptions of their parents' strengths and weaknesses are very strongly linked to their own self-appraisals. Finally, we identify several areas of future inquiry that directly address theories about the processes that contribute to both change and stability in the family environment.

Conceptual Framework and Methodological Rationale

The impetus for designing Dialogues About Families came from two sources: (1) a review of research on the family, revealing that reports by children are only rarely included and (2) a review of research in the areas of self-reflection and metacognition that highlights the central role and potentially mediating influence that children's perceptions have in their lives. Since children are difficult to assess with the methods commonly utilized with adults (for example, paper-and-pencil questionnaires, open-ended questions), we developed a Vygotskian-style dialogue method for interviewing young children about themselves, their parents, and their social networks. Considerable emphasis has been placed on assessing the reliability and validity of this dialogue method for interviewing young children, especially children who vary in temperament (for example, shyness and distractibility), reading and language skills, and family context. The results of these investigations as well as some of the insightful, contextually rich information provided by children are included in this chapter.

The conceptual framework guiding the content of these dialogues is a broad social-ecological perspective on families (see Landesman, Jaccard, and Gunderson, in press, for further elaboration). This model draws heavily from theoretical advances in developmental psychology, family therapy, sociology, and anthropology and includes four major elements: (1) goals and values, (2) strategies to realize goals, (3) resources, both physical and social, available to the family, and (4) individual experiences and behavioral qualities of family members. This conception is referred to as the GSRI model of family development to indicate the four major elements (goals, strategies, resources, and individuals). Many of the items in Dialogues About Families reflect these important areas of family life.

Central to the GSRI model is the assumption that individuals' perceptions mediate, to a considerable degree, their present and future behavior, which in turn may alter their socioemotional environments.

Guided by this model, Dialogues About Families was designed to assess *families as systems*. Specifically, each of the child dialogues has a parallel (self-administered) adult instrument that yields data suitable for comparing and combining family members' perceptions. The use of Dialogues About Families along with parental instruments provides the first opportunity, to our knowledge, to gather psychometrically robust data from all family members about comparable perceptions of one another, their social support, and their goals and values (see Exhibit 1). (Companion tools for direct observation of families and for observer ratings of family members and their relationships have been developed and used in

Exhibit 1. Basic Assumptions Underlying Dialogues About Families

1. *Events, perceptions, and reports of events are not synonymous.* Objective events that occur within the family and the perception of these events are not identical, for either children or adults. Further, when family members report on what occurs within the family, additional transformations are expected. These transformations are attributable in part to individual variables (see assumption 3) and in part to the contexts in which the reporting occurs.

2. *Perceptions are important to a family's functioning and developmental course.* Perceptions affect the development of individuals and the social contexts in which individuals operate. Actual events and the perceptions of the events by family members are assumed to influence the consequences of the events. In turn, both the events and their perceptions contribute to the developmental course of the family unit. "Perceptions" here are conceptualized broadly to include the particular experiences remembered, the duration and salience of those memories, the meaning ascribed to the events, the affective connotation of the events and experiences, and the substantiative details individuals provide when reporting about family events and experiences.

3. *Individuals have predispositions that affect their perceptions.* In principle, many individual variables predispose individual family members to particular biases in how they perceive behavioral events and in how willing they are to report on their experiences. These individual variables include developmental (for example, age, prior experience, and level of cognitive and emotional maturity) and normative (for example, cohort, gender, and role) components, as well as person-specific and idiographic elements (for example, personality or temperamental orientations, biological influences, and intelligence).

4. *Perceptions about major dimensions of family functioning are relatively stable, except during periods of disruption and change.* Reports of perceptions held by individual family members show reasonable stability and cohesion, especially when their families are functioning in ways they perceive as typical.

5. *Perceptions can be transformed into events.* When perceptions of family members about their family and one another are shared, the perceptions are transformed into behavioral events, which then are subject to further perceptions. Family members share their perceptions both directly and indirectly with one another, sometimes shortly after an event, other times far removed from the actual time of the event. The sharing of family members' experiences becomes an integral part of the family's behavior.

the Seattle Family Behavior Study. See Reid and Landesman [1989] and Landesman and Jaccard [1985]. These two tools serve the collection of independent perspectives on family members' expression of behavioral qualities, social support, and goals. Both tools are available from Sharon Landesman Ramey on request.)

To be sure, developmental inquiry about children's perceptions of their families has been limited by many difficulties, including developmental characteristics of children themselves. Foremost are the challenges presented by children's rapidly changing cognitive and verbal skills. As a result of these changes, instruments suitable for one age are not suitable for another. Using different measures to study children of different ages often obscures developmental transformations.

Children also vary considerably in their ease and enthusiasm in conversing with adults. The range in sociability, evident even when differences in both general and verbal intelligence are controlled, is another important factor that affects children's responses. Additional factors include children's distractibility, especially on self-administered instruments or those that do not provide personally engaging materials, as well as the markedly idiosyncratic ways children interpret items and questions. Rarely do existing assessment tools permit checking for children's attention and exploring children's comprehension so that the task presentation or the scoring can accommodate these differences.

Finally, children differ significantly in their ability to abstract and to engage in "what if" games. These differences limit the utility of projective techniques for understanding a child's perceptions of his or her family and selective relationships. Just as importantly, children's responses to open-ended questions frequently are fascinating, but rarely are they reliable and amenable to systematic comparison across children. That is, the failure to mention something spontaneously does not mean that an event or experience either has not occurred or is not important to a child.

All of the above characteristics of children's test behavior were considered in formulating Dialogues About Families. The method we developed to interview young children is based largely on work by Vygotsky (1978), who recognized that successful interviews with children utilize a basic dialogue unit, rather than a monologue, and engage children as active collaborators. These interviews do not rely on paper-and-pencil tasks, use of open-ended questions, children's verbal and academic skills, or projective techniques. Further, every session involves monitoring the child's level of understanding and engagement in the task. Each instrument in Dialogues About Families consists of related *dialogue stems*. Children responded to these dialogue stems by manipulating props (for example, picture cards, a ranking board, and a barometer with a movable marker to indicate "amount"), which facilitate focused attention and understandability. Throughout the assessment, children have the opportunity to ask questions, and the examiner determines each child's level of understanding at the beginning and the end of the session.

In addition, assessment of children's perceptions of families must be sensitive to human subjects' concerns, including the need for (1) exercising caution in probing about potential unhappiness, distress, and dissatisfaction; (2) obtaining informed consent from both parents and children; (3) establishing rapport and trust, so children are not reluctant to share actual feelings and perceptions; and (4) training examiners in how to handle any child reports indicative of possible neglect, abuse, or serious distortions. These concerns are as important to address in the study of normally developing children as they are in the study of exceptional children and high-risk families. (Children and parents must be informed in advance of the sessions that any possible signs of neglect or abuse of any family member will be reported to the appropriate authorities in a manner consistent with state guidelines.)

Collectively, Dialogues About Families provides an opportunity for systematically mapping children's emerging perceptions of self and of other family members and for delineating the mediating role of these perceptions in the development of children's social, emotional, and cognitive competencies. The information provided by children during these systematic child dialogues provides a complementary and distinct perspective to that obtained through parent interviews and ratings, direct behavioral observations, and standardized family assessments. Moreover, Dialogues About Families has utilized Vygotskian interactive methodology to probe areas of family development delineated in social-ecological theory and empirical research during the 1980s. Each instrument was constructed to accommodate supplementary dialogue stems specifically related to other theoretical or clinical areas of interest.

Description of Dialogues and Their Psychometric Properties

"What I'm Like and What Others in My Family Are Like." This tool consists of two parts: Part A is the child's self-description on a set of behavioral dimensions; Part B is the child's evaluation of mother, father, sibling(s), and other(s) on the same dimensions. The behavioral dimensions in this instrument typically are referred to as temperament or personality; their selection, however, was based on empirical work that indicated that these qualities were highly valued by parents of children five to fourteen years of age. In 1985, Landesman, Jaccard, and Reid conducted an intensive study of fifty-two heterogeneous families, randomly selected (telephone screening) to represent different types of middle-class families. In their homes, mothers and fathers were interviewed individually (with an average interview time of seventy-five minutes).

They identified qualities in their own children that they viewed as "most positive" and "most negative." Parents provided behavioral examples of how their children expressed these qualities, traits, or characteristics. From a content analysis of parents' responses involving category identification and individual response classification by four independent raters, the investigators identified behavioral qualities that were highly salient and important to the majority (over 65 percent) of parents. Parents expressed their commitment to promoting positive qualities, as well as to minimizing negative qualities. Further, when asked about current problems, parents spontaneously mentioned these same child behavioral qualities more frequently than any others. Accordingly, the investigators constructed an instrument based on behavioral dimensions highly valued by parents, both mothers and fathers, in a population-based cohort, rather than using an arbitrary set of temperament or personality variables. Ratings by children and parents of themselves and other family members in terms of these valued qualities may be sensitive to mediating factors that relate to a family's overall functioning and success. Table 1 lists these behavioral qualities in their positive and negative terms, as described by parents and children.

To determine whether children have a good understanding of these parent-valued characteristics, Reid and Landesman conducted a pilot study of sixty-five children (four to fourteen years of age) and learned that the behavioral dimensions "organized," "flexible (not stubborn)," "emotionally stable," and "outgoing/friendly" were not well understood by the children, especially those under eight years of age. Accordingly, the children's own terms and examples of the ten positive qualities in Table 2 are included in the final version of "What I'm Like and What Others in My Family Are Like."

In Part A, "What I'm Like," the examiner orients the child to the session and shows the child ten cards, each presenting a behavioral quality in either word or picture form (depending on the child's reading level). The examiner adapts the following introduction to the child's developmental level: "Here are cards that show some things parents really like about young people your age. Almost all young people have some or all of these things, like being happy or being helpful. We would like you to use these cards to tell us about *yourself.*" The child is given an opportunity to explore the props and ask questions. Children are assured their answers will remain confidential: "I won't tell anyone about your answers, because they are your answers and feelings, *unless* you tell me something that could be harmful to you or someone else." In addition to cards, other props are a wooden ranking board into which the cards are inserted and a rating barometer with key labels and a red, movable level-indicator. Similar props are used in the other child dialogue instruments, with appropriate changes on the barometer's labels to reflect the content

Table 1. Behavioral Qualities Most Highly Valued by Middle-Class Parents of Children Five to Fourteen Years of Age and Their Children's Definitions

Parents' Terms Positive (and Opposite)	Children's Terms
Cooperative/helpful (noncompliant/unhelpful)	I am helpful
Creative (unimaginative/lacks spontaneity)	I am good at finding new ways to do things
Emotionally stable (emotionally volatile)	(Non-reliable data)
Flexible (stubborn/non-adaptable)	(Non-reliable data)
Happy (sad)	I am cheerful
Honest (deceitful)	I tell the truth and don't hide things
Independent/able to do things on own (dependent/clings to parent)	I can do things on my own
Inquisitive/eager to learn (lacks curiosity)	I like to try new things
Loving/affectionate (aloof)	I am a loving person who shows people how much I care about them
Outgoing/friendly (shy/withdrawn)	(Non-reliable data)
Organized (disorganized/scattered)	(Non-reliable data)
Responsible/trustworthy (undependable/unreliable)	People can trust me to do things
Self-confident/likes self (insecure/has low self-esteem)	I like myself and know I am good at doing things
Sensitive/caring (insensitive to others)	I think about how other people feel

of each dialogue. Figure 1 shows a sample of six cards, the ranking board, and the barometer.

After initial orientation, the examiner asks the child to place the card with the quality that describes him or her "the very best" in the first slot of the ranking board. Then the examiner asks the child to look at the remaining cards, distributed on a table top in front of the child, and to select the card that describes him or her "the second best" or "next best." This line of inquiry proceeds until all cards are ranked. Following the rank ordering of the qualities, the examiner probes the child about "how much" of each behavioral quality he or she has "compared to other children your same age." The examiner reminds the child "that there are no right or wrong answers" and "I am interested in how you really feel

Figure 1. Props Used to Administer "What I'm Like and What Others in My Family Are Like"

and think." The child uses the indicator on the barometer to indicate how much of each quality he or she perceives in himself or herself. The 60-point scale ranges from -30, which is "a whole lot less than other children my age," to +30, which indicates "a whole lot more than other children." The session summary for each subject contains both a ranking and a rating on each behavioral quality. This summary indicates (1) the salience and importance of certain behavioral qualities to the child's perception of "self" and (2) the child's sense of self-worth, via his or her quantitative descriptions in comparison to other children. Such data provide an opportunity for systematic study of children's perceptions of their *most* and *least* distinguishing characteristics, as well as overall positive self-appraisals. When parallel instruments are used in which parents rank and rate their children on the same dimensions, a broader perspective on children's individual differences can be obtained. From the family profile data, a variety of theoretically important quantitative indices can be generated, including estimates of perceived similarities and differences among family members, for either select dyads or the entire family; scores of overall positive appraisal of the child; and major discrepancies in perceptions of self versus others.

Part B, "What Others in My Family Are Like," is constructed in a fashion parallel to Part A. The examiner asks the child to arrange (rank) the cards in the order that best describes the other family member in question (for example, mother, father, sibling) from most salient (for example, "When you think about your mother, which one of these cards is the *best* way to describe her?") to least salient. Then, the child uses the barometer to rate each family member on all qualities, comparing the family member to others who play the same role (for example, "How happy do you think your mother is, *compared to other mothers?*").

A study of the psychometric properties of "What I Am Like and What Others in My Family Are Like" indicates that children provide reliable reports on themselves and their parents. A population-based study of 339 children (148 boys, 191 girls; 269 white, 70 black), ranging from six to twelve years of age (see Reid and Landesman, 1989), involved administering the dialogues to children, in their homes, twice within a four-week period by the same examiner. Test-retest correlations of the children's overall appraisals were .71 for overall descriptions of self, .71 for mother, and .73 for father. Test-retest reliability also was examined using the kappa statistic, which corrects "agreement by chance." The kappas indicate that the stability of children's rankings was higher for the first three (.78, .52, and .49) and last two qualities (.53 and .67) than for the middle-ranked qualities ($M = .33$). These findings indicate that children's self-appraisals yield a pattern similar to adults', with highest reliabilities for qualities they feel describe them the "best" and "least" (see Reid, Landesman, Jaccard, and Rabkin, 1987).

In a manner recommended by Harter and Pike (1984), we queried children after the completion of the instrument about their understanding of each behavioral quality. An independent content analysis by independent raters of children's open-ended responses revealed that more than 95 percent of the children had good comprehension and understanding of the behavioral dimensions that they had been ranking and rating for themselves and their parents. Children generally provided highly specific and perceptive responses that revealed keen observations of the expression of these qualities in their own and their parents' behaviors. Examples of the personalized nature of some of the children's responses include "I know my dad is *independent* because when something breaks he always says 'let's try to fix it ourselves' (before asking for help)," "My mom is *responsible* because when she carpools she always get us there *on time*," and "I am a *creative* person because I want to be an actress and I make up plays in my head when I walk home from school." Not surprisingly, the reasons children provide for descriptions of themselves are frequently linked to the recognition they have received from significant others (for example, "I know I am *honest* because my mom tells me that I am," and "I got an award for being the most *loving* child in the gym when a student got hurt, therefore I know I am loving").

It is interesting that children's perceptions of their parents are related not only (egocentrically) to instances of parental behavior toward them (for example, "My dad is *loving* because he hugs and kisses *me*") but also to the children's observations of their parents' behavior toward others, both inside and outside the home (for example, "My dad is *eager to learn* because he is in business for himself and is always learning new things, like computer programming," and "I know my parents are *loving* people because they love each other"). The advances in social cognition that occur during the middle childhood period were illustrated in a number of the children's responses in which an understanding of less readily apparent or more subtle aspects of behavioral expression was revealed. For example, several children said that a parent who is *loving* "remains fair even when angry [with me]." Additionally, in describing self-confidence, several children mentioned that self-confident people "let others know what they got wrong as well as what they got right."

"My Family and Friends." This instrument yields information about children's reports of (1) perceived availability of individuals in their networks to provide different types of social support and (2) their satisfaction with the help they receive. The content of the dialogues is based on research with adults, emphasizing the differentiation of social support into four types (emotional, informational, instrumental, and companionship support; see Cohen and Willis, 1985), and on empirical work with children, focusing on the importance of emotional security (Bretherton and Waters, 1985). In addition, one dialogue stem concerns conflict, since

even close supportive relationships may involve anger and negative interactions (Berndt and Perry, 1986; Braiker and Kelly, 1979; Furman and
Buhrmester, 1985). "My Family and Friends" consists of twelve dialogue
stems that cover the following social situations: (1) sharing positive and
negative feelings, (2) pleasure at success, (3) doing something bad, (4)
feeling understood, (5) feeling admired, (6) wanting to learn something,
(7) needing information, (8) needing help with schoolwork, (9) needing
help with chores, (10) being with someone who makes you feel happy,
(11) doing fun things, and (12) getting upset (for details, see Reid and
Landesman, 1988).

"My Family and Friends" begins with the child identifying the key
persons in his or her active social network. Cards with each person's
name are written; for very young or developmentally delayed children,
drawings or photographs can be used. The examiner introduces the session as follows: "All of us talk to or go to different people for different
things. Right now, I would like to know whom you turn to when you
want different things, and what that is like for you." A wooden ranking
board and large rating barometer (similar to the one pictured in Figure
1, but with labels corresponding to the content of the social support dialogues) are incorporated as props.

For each dialogue stem, the examiner asks the child to place the
name cards in the ranking board, one at a time, in an order indicating to
whom the child goes first, second, and so on in a particular social support situation. For example, the child may be asked, "If you did something that you felt really bad about, that no one knew about, who [sic]
would you talk to?" or "When you want to just 'hang out' or do really
fun things, who [sic] do you go to first?" After ranking the cards, the
child uses the barometer to rate how satisfied he or she is with the support received from each individual. The examiner then inquires, "When
you talk to your brother when you're feeling 'badly,' how much better do
you feel?" or "When you go to your father for information, how much
do you really learn?"

The social support data are scored in terms of the prioritization of
whom the child turns to for each type of support and how satisfied the
child is with each type of support received from each person. Additional
summary scores include an average level of satisfaction with each type of
social support (regardless of who provides the support), an overall summary score for each person in the network, satisfaction ratings for each
person across the four types of support, and a total conflict score. When
data from the parallel parental report "Your Child's Social Network" are
gathered, then scores can be computed to indicate the nature and degree
of concordance (versus discrepancy) between children's and parents' perceptions of the child's social network. Further, similarities between how
parents and children perceive their *own* social networks can be examined.

(Information and documentation of other, parallel social support instruments for parents can be obtained from the authors.)

The test construction of "My Family and Friends" involved a study similar to that for "What I'm Like and What Others in My Family Are Like" and is described in detail elsewhere (Reid, Landesman, Treder, and Jaccard, 1989). Briefly, use of "My Family and Friends" in a population-based study of 249 children (105 boys, 144 girls; 205 white, 44 black), ranging from six to twelve years of age, yielded relatively reliable and valid reports about the quality of and differentiation within their social support networks. The intraclass test-retest correlations for rankings and ratings were .68 for rankings and .69 for ratings, which are in the acceptable "high moderate" range for social and personality inventories with children. The internal consistency of the support types was satisfactory, M Cronbach alpha = .72. The alphas were the highest for the five emotional dialogue stems, with all scores greater than .72. The internal consistency was higher for children's ratings of family members (M Cronbach alpha = .77) than for their ratings of nonfamily members (M Cronbach alpha = .61).

Additionally, a repeated-measures analysis of variance on children's responses detected significant effects for the type of social support ($F[2.75,440.48] = 86.07$, $p < .001$), the source of support ($F[3.28,525.02] = 69.29$, $p < .001$), and the interaction between support type and source ($F[8.30,1328.44] = 135.76$, $p < .001$). These findings support the conclusion that children's reports differ as a function of both who is rated and what type of social support is considered. Thus, from at least six years old and beyond, children reliably distinguish differences in the ability of particular individuals to provide specific types of social support to them.

A listing of children's own descriptions of their emotional, informational, instrumental, and affiliative needs is reported elsewhere (Reid, Landesman, Treder, and Jaccard, 1989). Children's responses were consistent with the general definitions of social support provided by Cohen and Willis (1985), yet the responses provided personalized insights into the many highly specific, day-to-day social support needs of children. Especially noteworthy were the serious concerns children expressed in relation to their informational needs. Middle childhood is characterized by rapid expansion and acquisition of knowledge. In addition to learning school-related information, numerous children expressed needs to learn about personal safety and world events.

"My Family and Friends" was designed with an expandable format, so that modifications for use with clinical and special populations can be made readily. The sensitivity of the instrument has encouraged its use in research that identifies sources of risk and protection in the responses of young children (see Cauce, Reid, Landesman, and Gonzales, in press).

In particular, profile analysis of a child's social support has been used to identify salient support sources that may contribute to children's resilience, as well as deficits in support that potentially put the child at-risk socially or emotionally. Cases of support deficits include children who report seeking help from their parents but continually feel very disappointed with the minimal help received and children who report having no friends or siblings in whom to confide.

"What Is Important in My Family." This instrument is a relatively brief dialogue that probes the child's perceptions of family goals and priorities. The five major goal domains of family functioning identified were selected because of their theoretical significance for parenting activities and for child outcomes. These major goal domains were confirmed by a pilot study in which parents spontaneously mentioned goals and values that clustered in these areas. The five goal areas are (1) *fostering personal ("character") development:* helping family members acquire beliefs, attitudes, and behavioral orientations adaptable across a variety of life situations; (2) *careproviding:* providing for family members' physical needs and promoting health; (3) *promoting within-family relationships:* establishing and maintaining positive interpersonal relationships in the family; (4) *educating and training:* fostering academic skills, as well as facilitating skills related to future vocational competence; and (5) *maintaining societal norms and order:* encouraging family members to function cooperatively outside the family and helping them understand cultural norms, expectations, and laws.

In administering "What Is Important in My Family," the examiner talks with the child about a set of cards depicting the five goal areas of family functioning. The examiner says, "Here are some cards that show things families feel are important to do. Let's look at these pictures carefully and think about what they mean." The child then provides examples of how families might encourage each of their children (1) "to try to be a good person, to live a good life, and to do what is important," (2) "to be healthy and keep their home nice," (3) "to love and get along with people in their own family," (4) "to do 'good' in school and to learn as much as they can about how the world works," and (5) "to know the rules and manner for getting along with others outside their family; to be a good citizen."

In Part A, "What I Think Is Important in Families," the examiner asks the child to select the card that depicts the goal "which you, *yourself,* think is the *most* important thing for families to do" and to place that goal card in the first slot of the ranking board. This continues until all cards are ranked. Then the child rates the importance of each area, using the barometer. In Part B, "What Others in My Family Think Is Important," the child's perceptions of the importance of these family goals to each parent are obtained. The child is encouraged to "Look at the cards and think about how important each of these goals or activities is to your (mother/father)." Then the child is asked to "Select the card that you think your (mother/father) would say is the most important thing for families to do." The child proceeds to rank all cards and then to complete a rating for each card to answer "How important do you think (goal area) is to your (mother/father)?"

Developmental Patterns in Children's Perceptions of Their Families and Themselves

As "first-hand reporters," children provide well-differentiated and highly personalized reports of themselves, family members, and their relationships. Figure 2 presents children's mean ratings of self, mother, and father on the ten personality/temperament characteristics from "What I Am Like and What Others in My Family Are Like." On average, children rated themselves highest on "loving" and "creative," rated their mothers highest on "loving" and "honest," and described their fathers as highest on "loving" and "independent." Note that children tended to rate their parents higher than themselves on all qualities except "eager to learn" and "creative," two areas in which they rated their mothers the lowest.

Table 2 reports the developmental trends found in children's appraisals of self, mother, and father. Age differences were examined by conducting multivariate analyses of variance, followed by one-way analyses of variance when the MANOVA was significant. In most of the analyses, the developmental trends were examined by comparing children six to nine years of age (early elementary school) with those ten to twelve years of age (preadolescent), because these age groups correspond to two theoretically important age groups within the middle childhood period. The preadolescents, in contrast to the younger children, had significantly less positive appraisals of themselves ($F[10,327] = 2.42$, $p = .0085$), their mothers ($F[10,326] = 3.14$, $p = .0008$), and their fathers ($F[10,170] = 2.21$, $p = .0192$) across the ten qualities. Self-appraisals of creativity and eagerness to learn showed particularly large declines across the two age groups, although the children did not rate their parents lower on these qualities as a function of their own age. In contrast, the two areas in which the children's perceptions showed large shifts concerned how happy and loving they saw their mothers and fathers. What would be especially important to study are potential behavioral correlates associated with children's shifts in how they perceive parents and in their own self-esteem. Further, the degree to which parents' perceptions of their children shift across these age periods would be valuable to delineate, particularly in relation to objective events and to their own children's self-appraisals. For example, are parents' perceptions of their children highly correlated with their children's own perceptions?

**Figure 2. Children's Mean Ratings of Self, Mother, and Father
from the Dialogue "What I Am Like and What Others
in My Family Are Like"**

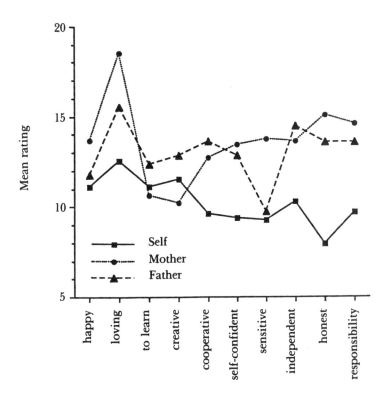

Another developmental change in the children's perceptions was the declining ratings of their mothers' honesty. Theoretically, this may be a function of children's increased social cognitive capacities, especially the ability to perceive relationships in less absolute and more multifaceted ways (Flavell, 1982; Selman, 1980). Another potential contributor to this developmental shift may be the "natural" disillusionment that social psychologists hypothesize occurs across time in any relationship. Also, a less uniformly positive and more critical stance toward one's parents has been hypothesized as necessary for "differentiation" of self and successful adolescent development (Loevinger, 1976; Marcia, 1976).

Table 3 displays the mean support and conflict ratings that children provided for each relationship, based on "My Family and Friends." The

Table 2. Mean Ratings of Self, Mother, and Father by
Children Six to Nine and Ten to Twelve Years of Age

Quality	Self		Mother		Father	
	6–9 (N=161)	10–12 (N=177)	6–9 (N=161)	10–12 (N=176)	6–9 (N=82)	10–12 (N=99)
Cooperative	10.80 (12.60)	8.56 (10.77)	13.15 (14.02)	11.83 (11.48)	15.11 (13.03)	12.35 (11.51)
Creative	13.52 (13.32)	9.75 (12.32)	9.67 (15.25)	10.23 (13.70)	11.91 (16.66)	13.61 (13.19)
Happy	12.06 (12.61)	10.23 (12.01)	15.87 (12.00)	11.69 (12.08)	13.22 (12.98)	10.52 (11.24)
Honest	8.60 (15.66)	5.90 (11.27)	17.24 (13.56)	13.09 (12.11)	13.48 (13.01)	13.59 (11.45)
Independent	10.46 (14.41)	10.02 (11.10)	14.65 (13.06)	12.62 (11.89)	15.21 (13.94)	13.85 (11.36)
Eager to learn	14.02 (14.63)	8.44 (12.79)	11.09 (14.56)	10.13 (12.24)	12.16 (14.34)	12.49 (13.25)
Loving	14.14 (13.39)	11.06 (11.05)	21.20 (10.70)	16.01 (10.61)	17.41 (13.10)	13.94 (11.04)
Responsible	11.72 (13.87)	7.83 (11.00)	15.28 (12.91)	13.87 (12.08)	14.85 (13.25)	12.42 (12.00)
Self-confident	10.35 (13.69)	8.50 (12.08)	15.20 (12.98)	11.76 (11.37)	14.70 (13.22)	11.24 (10.45)
Sensitive	10.19 (14.56)	8.44 (12.35)	14.65 (14.78)	12.88 (11.03)	8.46 (15.37)	10.75 (11.97)

Note: Parenthetical values are standard deviations of means. Ratings are on a 60-point scale ranging from –30 to +30.

multivariate approach to repeated-measures analysis was used to determine the extent to which the children's reports of perceived support and conflict varied as a function of the social relationship and the child's age. Separate MANOVAs were conducted for each type of support and for conflict. When the MANOVA for relationship × age was significant, all possible pairwise comparisons of sources of support were conducted to determine which types of social relationships were perceived as providing more support.

Significant relationship effects were found for all four areas of support and for conflict: emotional ($F[2,236] = 198$, $p < .0001$), instrumental ($F[2,236] = 254$, $p < .0001$), informational ($F[2,236] = 172$, $p < .0001$), companionship ($F[2,236] = 212$, $p < .0001$), and conflict ($F[2,236] = 150$, $p < .0001$). These findings indicate that children can recognize distinct social support resources within their social networks. (Due to space limitations, only multivariate test statistics are provided here. However, all

Table 3. Children's Mean Satisfaction Ratings of
Social Support and Conflict by Relationship

Relationship	Emotional	Informational	Instrumental	Companionship	Conflict
Parent	42.21	43.02	42.10	41.21	28.53
(N = 339)	(7.22)	(7.03)	(7.47)	(9.26)	(15.46)
Sibling	28.68	23.01	25.57	33.69	41.07
(N = 242)	(12.39)	(15.61)	(14.28)	(12.54)	(11.94)
Friend	34.88	24.89	22.86	43.21	20.82
(N = 337)	(10.01)	(13.41)	(13.16)	(7.64)	(11.94)
Relative	32.30	28.98	21.89	35.77	14.47
(N = 285)	(11.80)	(15.11)	(16.41)	(13.18)	(15.62)
Teacher	25.63	40.56	22.15	18.83	23.91
(N = 336)	(12.47)	(10.02)	(10.37)	(16.34)	(17.08)

Note: When a child had more than one person in a given provider category, then the person rated the highest or most salient was used to calculate the means. Parenthetical values are standard deviations of means. Ratings are on a 51-point scale from 0 to 50.

comparisons among the types of relationships documented in Table 3 were significant [$p < .05$].)

In general, the children perceived their parents to be the best multipurpose providers in their individual networks of social support. Parents tended to be viewed as the best source of emotional, informational (along with teachers), and instrumental support. Not surprisingly, friends were seen as a good source of companionship and were rated significantly better in this area than parents, siblings, and teachers. Friends also were rated highly on emotional support (second only to parents); however, they generally were not perceived as a good source of informational and instrumental assistance.

The children perceived their siblings as a good source of general companionship, unlike teachers, who were rated as a good source of information about "how the world works," but as a relatively poor source of fun companionship and emotional support. Children's ratings for perceived conflict showed a quite different pattern. Siblings were rated as the source of most conflict, parents and teachers next highest, and friends as the least likely source of conflict.

Significant age × relationship interactions were found for emotional support ($F[2,326] = 12.2$, $p < .0001$), companionship support ($F[2,326] = 8.2$, $p < .0001$), and conflict ($F[2,326] = 5.1$, $p < .01$). Specifically, developmental differences were found in children's perceptions of the emotional support, companionship, and conflict they experience with teachers and friends. While children of all ages perceived their teachers as a good source of informational support, only the children six to nine years of age perceived their teachers as a good source of emotional support and companionship. In contrast, preadolescent children clearly preferred their parents and friends over teachers as sources of emotional support and companionship. Similarly, the preadolescent children perceived their relationships with their teachers to be significantly more conflictual than did the younger children. This is consistent with teachers' and parents' reports that during the early elementary school years, children very much want their teachers to like them, and they tend to see teachers as friends or perhaps as mother surrogates. However, as they approach adolescence, strong positive attachments with teachers seem to decline for the majority.

These developmental findings about children's relationships with their parents and friends corroborate work by others (for example, Berndt and Perry, 1986; Cauce, 1986; Furman and Buhrmester, 1985; Hunter and Youniss, 1982), although the present data involve younger children and provide a more detailed profile of children's social support and self-ratings. In particular, the findings from our sample (kindergarten to sixth-grade children) extend the findings from Hunter and Youniss' (1982) sample (fourth- to tenth-grade children), suggesting that within the period spanning from early childhood through adolescence, the level of support and intimacy with parents remains relatively constant, while intimacy with friends increases with age.

Table 4 shows children's ratings of the importance of family goals for themselves and their parents during the dialogue "What Is Important in My Family." Children rated "having good family relationships" as the most important family goal for themselves and for their mothers, while they perceived "educational/vocational goals" as being the most important to their fathers. Rather surprising was the fact that no significant developmental differences were found in children's ratings of goals. Table 4 provides select examples of children's conceptions of each goal area, based on systematic probes. Overall, more than 90 percent of the children provided examples clearly relevant to each goal area.

In sum, the children's perceptions of their families speak to the centrality of family members in their social support networks. The children perceived high amounts of positive social support from their parents and strongly endorsed the importance of within-family relationships as a major goal. However, for the older age groups, the reported relationships with adults (both parents and teachers) in their lives became less uniformly positive and more differentiated. Similarly, during later middle childhood, children reported having more complex appraisals of their *own* strengths and weaknesses, as rated relative to their peers. The reported sibling relationships are noteworthy for their high degree of both affiliation and conflict. And friends were reported to be a good source of emotional support and companionship. Moreover, as we move from the younger children to the preadolescents, the increasing value of friendships did not decrease the importance they assigned to receiving emotional support, information, and direct assistance from their parents.

Table 4. Percentage of Children Ranking Each of the Five Domains of Family Functioning as First, with Select Examples

Domain	For Self	For Mother	For Father	Examples
Fostering personal ("character") development	24.5	14.7	19.2	"Be nice and kind to other people" "Think about how others feel" "Always do the best I can" "Always try to do what is right" "Do what's important to me"
Providing care	12.0	21.5	14.3	"Brush my teeth or exercise" "Make my bed and pick up my room" "Eat the right foods, like vegetables" "Put in a fire alarm even though it costs money"
Promoting within-family relationships	28.0	30.4	22.0	"Share and get along with each other" "Try not to fight with my brother or take his things" "Give hugs and kisses and say 'I love you'" "Hang out together" "Sit down and talk with mom if I have a problem"
Education and training	16.8	21.8	30.2	"Study every day and do homework" "Read books and go to the library" "Try my hardest to do well" "Listen to mom tell stories of kids who didn't do well in school"
Maintaining societal norms and order	18.6	11.2	14.2	"Be polite and considerate" "Think about others first, take turns" "Keep friends for a long time" "Know how your city or country is doing and vote"

Note: The examples represent the responses most frequently given during the content validity study.

Interdependencies Among Children's Subjective Appraisals

Analyses were conducted to examine how the children's perceptions related to different aspects of their families. In particular, we explored the ways in which children's self-appraisals, perceptions of parents, and overall satisfaction with emotional support were related in order to evaluate a central assumption in the GSRI framework of how families function: perceptions of self and others and of the adequacy of social resources are interlinked, due to the presence of reciprocal influences in the family (see Hinde and Stevenson-Hinde, 1987, 1988). First, simple correlations were conducted between self-appraisals and children's reported satisfaction with the emotional support they received from all of their relationships (corrected for different sizes of children's social networks). We selected emotional support to illustrate this interdependency principle, in part because research on infants and toddlers suggests that emotional support or security is related to later autonomy and the child's sense of self (Bretherton, 1985; Sroufe and Fleeson, 1986), and because so little is known about emotional bonds and self-perception during middle childhood. Also, we had learned in prior analyses (Reid, Landesman, Treder, and Jaccard, 1989) that ratings of emotional support correlated highly with the other types of support: with companionship ($r = .74$, $p < .0001$); with instrumental help ($r = .69$, $p < .0001$); and with informational assistance ($r = .71$, $p < .0001$). The correlation of $r = .41$ ($p < .0001$) between children's perceptions of total emotional support and their own self-appraisals supports an interpretation that children's views of their own behavior are intimately linked to their perceptions of the support they receive from others. A similar correlation of $r = .42$ ($p < .0001$) was found between children's perceptions of social support from their mothers and their own self-appraisals; the correlation between perceived social support from their fathers and positive self-image is of comparable magnitude ($r = .38$, $p < .0001$).

Next, we considered how similar children's ratings of themselves and their parents were for the ten behavioral qualities. The correlation between self-appraisal and mother appraisal was $r = .65$ ($p < .0001$), and between self-appraisal and father appraisal $r = .65$ ($p < .0001$), suggesting that children's perceptions of themselves are linked, as hypothesized, to their impressions of their parents.

This set of intercorrelations indicates that children's perceptions are not neatly compartmentalized during middle childhood. Further analyses support the nonindependence of family goals, child and family characteristics, and developmental and social conditions. That is, we found interesting statistical associations among children's reported perceptions of themselves and their perceptions of significant others within their social worlds. What remains to be understood are the developmental pathways contributing to these linkages and how these influence the responses of children and parents to one another's behavior.

Concluding Remarks and Future Directions

This chapter describes Dialogues About Families, a new methodology for obtaining personalized family information from children. With a presentation format based on cognitive developmental theory and designed for application across a wide developmental age range, psychometrically robust data on perceptions of the family and self can be collected. The contents emanate from a family systems perspective and address three important areas in child and family development: attributions about valued qualities in self and parents, perceptions of diverse types of social support, and appraisals of family goals and values. Parallel adult instruments complement the information obtained from children and permit a synthesis of data to profile the family as a unit.

The rationale underlying Dialogues About Families is that (1) both behavioral events and the perceptions of those events (for example, interpretations and memories of the events and their salience for family members) influence the consequences of events and the evolution of the family as a system and (2) individual family members vary in how they perceive behavioral events due to individual and developmental variables, such as age, birth order, gender, cohort, individual history, biological influences, and personality or temperament. The rich variation in individual family members' interpretations of events and the role of these perceptions in motivating future family behavior underscore the need for reliable and systematic methods for interviewing all family members about critical aspects of family life.

The chapter provides an overview of the administration of Dialogues About Families with young children. Children's reports indicate that they value family relationships, perceive their parents as an important source of support and assistance, and recognize differential strengths and weaknesses in their parents and in themselves. Siblings and friends are valued sources of companionship, although siblings (unlike friends) are also seen as a significant source of conflict. Appraisals of parents become more complex as children become older, and more instances of conflicts with parents are reported as children approach preadolescence.

We think that the sensitivity of Dialogues About Families to the child's viewpoint makes this a valuable method for studying families, especially for research on how children's perspectives can contribute to observed differences in their patterns of behavioral and emotional adjustment, both within and outside the family. When using both the child and the parallel adult instruments, Dialogues About Families provides, for the first time, an opportunity to gather systematic data from early childhood through adulthood and to simultaneously appraise all family members on the same dimensions. As a methodology, it allows us to examine family processes (1) cross-sectionally, by studying the interdependencies of people who are at different stages in the life cycle but are bound within the same family unit and (2) longitudinally, by charting the ontology of family processes.

The methods required to move "beyond the dyad" in family research and to gather, analyze, and interpret data from parents and their children are unavoidably time-consuming and complex. Yet, without such endeavors, profiles of families lack the dimensionality and mutually independent qualities that in principle characterize families and contribute significantly to child outcomes. When combined with behavioral methods, Dialogues About Families permits the examination of personalized meaning of events over time and leads us to a more dynamic understanding of families and the children that grow up in them.

References

Berndt, T. J., and Perry, T. B. "Children's Perceptions of Friendships as Supportive Relationships." *Developmental Psychology*, 1986, *22*, 640-648.

Braiker, H. B., and Kelly, H. H. "Conflict in the Development of Close Relationships." In R. L. Burgess and T. L. Huston (eds.), *Social Exchange in Developing Relationships*. New York: Academic Press, 1979.

Bretherton, I. "Attachment Theory: Retrospect and Prospect." In I. Bretherton and E. Waters (eds.), *Growing Points of Attachment: Theory and Research. Monographs of the Society for Research in Child Development*, 1985, *50* (1-2, serial no. 209).

Bretherton, I., and Waters, E. (eds.). *Growing Points of Attachment: Theory and Research. Monographs of the Society for Research in Child Development*, 1985, *50* (1-2, serial no. 209).

Cauce, A. M. "Social Networks and Social Competence: Exploring the Effects of Early Adolescent Friendships." *American Journal of Community Psychology*, 1986, *14*, 607-628.

Cauce, A. M., Reid, M., Landesman, S., and Gonzales, N. "Social Support in Young Children: Measurement, Description, and Behavioral Impact." In I. G. Sarason, B. R. Sarason, and G. Pierce (eds.), *Social Support: An Interactional Perspective*. New York: Wiley, in press.

Cohen, S., and Willis, T. A. "Stress, Social Support, and the Buffering Hypothesis." *Psychological Bulletin*, 1985, *98*, 310-357.

Flavell, J. H. "On Cognitive Development." *Child Development*, 1982, *53*, 1-10.

Furman, W., and Buhrmester, D. "Children's Perceptions of the Personal Relationships in Their Social Networks." *Developmental Psychology*, 1985, *21*, 1016-1024.

Harter, S., and Pike, R. "The Pictorial Scale of Perceived Competence and Social Acceptance for Young Children." *Child Development*, 1984, *55*, 1969-1982.

Hinde, R. A., and Stevenson-Hinde, J. "Interpersonal Relationships and Child Development." *Developmental Review*, 1987, *7*, 1-21.

Hinde, R. A., and Stevenson-Hinde, J. (eds.). *Relationships Within Families: Mutual Influences.* Oxford, England: Clarendon Press, 1988.

Hunter, F. T., and Youniss, J. "Changes in Functions of Three Relationships During Adolescence." *Developmental Psychology*, 1982, *18*, 806–811.

Landesman, S., and Jaccard, J. *Sources of Help for Parenting and Family Management.* Unpublished instrument, Department of Psychiatry and Behavioral Sciences, University of Washington, 1985.

Landesman, S., Jaccard, J., and Gunderson, V. "The Family Environment: The Combined Influence of Family Behavior, Goals, Strategies, Resources, and Individual Experiences." In M. Lewis and S. Feinman (eds.), *Social Influences and Socialization in Infancy.* New York: Plenum, in press.

Loevinger, J. *Ego Development: Conceptions and Theories.* San Francisco: Jossey-Bass, 1976.

Marcia, J. E. "Development and Validation of Ego Identity Status." *Journal of Personality and Social Psychology*, 1976, *3*, 551–558.

Reid, M., and Landesman, S. *Being a Family Member: Dialogues with Children.* Seattle: Department of Psychiatry and Behavioral Sciences, University of Washington, 1987.

Reid, M., and Landesman, S. *My Family and Friends, Preschool Version: A Social Support Dialogue Instrument for Children.* (Adapted for handicapped children.) Seattle: Department of Psychiatry and Behavioral Sciences, University of Washington, 1988.

Reid, M., and Landesman, S. *Parents' Social Networks.* Unpublished instrument, Department of Psychiatry and Behavioral Sciences, University of Washington, 1989.

Reid, M., Landesman, S., Jaccard, J., and Rabkin, J. "Dialogues with Children: The Child as Reporter for Family and Self." Paper presented at the meeting of the Society for Research in Child Development, Baltimore, Md., April 1987.

Reid, M., Landesman, S., Treder, R., and Jaccard, J. "My Family and Friends: 6–12-Year-Old Children's Perceptions of Social Support." *Child Development*, 1989, *60*, 896–910.

Selman, R. L. *The Growth of Interpersonal Understanding.* New York: Academic Press, 1980.

Sroufe, L. A., and Fleeson, J. "Attachment and the Construction of Relationships." In W. Hartup and Z. Rubin (eds.), *Relationships and Development.* Hillsdale, N.J.: Erlbaum, 1986.

Vygotsky, L. S. *Mind in Society: The Development of Higher Psychological Processes.* (M. Cole, V. John-Steiner, S. Scribner, and E. Souberman, eds. and trans.). Cambridge, Mass.: Harvard University Press, 1978.

Molly Reid is chief psychologist at the Child Development and Mental Retardation Center and assistant professor in the Department of Psychiatry and Behavioral Sciences at the University of Washington, Seattle.

Sharon Landesman Ramey is professor of psychiatry and psychology at the University of North Carolina, Chapel Hill, and director of the Frank Porter Graham Child Development Center.

Margaret Burchinal is an investigator at the Frank Porter Graham Child Development Center and adjunct assistant professor of psychology at the University of North Carolina, Chapel Hill.

Children's representations of so-called Oedipal conflicts among family members seem at first exacerbated and then later resolved by their changing conceptions of family role relationships.

Developmental Shifts in Oedipal Behaviors Related to Family Role Understanding

Malcolm W. Watson, Kenneth Getz

A four-year-old boy had been showing extra attention to his mother and wanting to sleep in her bed each night. When his mother told him that she loved him, he said, "And I love you too, and that's why I can't ever marry someone else." Such recurring comments and behaviors of preschool children suggest that some so-called Oedipal phenomena exist. Some sort of explanation of these phenomena is needed, even though many psychologists have rejected Freud's (1963, 1965) original, developmental account of the Oedipus complex because of the lack of objective support for its universality (see Malinowski, 1955; Spiro, 1982) and because of the difficulty in testing the underlying theory (see Pollock, 1986; Sears, 1942).

The four-year-old in the above example could have been driven by desires for the exclusive attention and sexual affection of his mother. He could also have been experiencing concurrent antagonistic and competitive thoughts toward his father, with the attendant feelings of fear and guilt, and thus could have been in the midst of a full-blown Oedipal conflict, as Freud theorized.

This research was supported by the John D. and Catherine T. MacArthur Foundation Network on Early Childhood Transitions. The authors thank Suzanne Wahler, Debra Hassenfeld, and Chris Boyatzis for their help in completing this study and Joseph Cunningham and Kurt Fischer for suggestions regarding the study.

However, there are other possible explanations for his emotional declaration of intent to marry. In thinking about the future when he might be required to leave his mother, especially if he were to marry someone else, he could have been wrestling with an impending sense of loss. How could he handle not being in the care of his mother? Because preschoolers have a difficult time conceiving of themselves and others in two or more roles simultaneously (Watson, 1984), we can postulate that, in this boy's mind, his only alternatives to being separated from the love and security of his parents, especially of his mother, were either to stay her son forever or, if he must grow up and get married (and thus no longer be a son), to marry his own mother and thus never have to leave her. Young children do learn quite early certain conceptions about their social worlds: We do grow up and usually leave our parents; we tend to marry the persons we love most; and males marry females (Fischer and Watson, 1983). Thus, when a boy, who is a male, loves his mother, who is a female, he just might marry her when he grows up and thus stave off his impending loss.

If this second explanation were in fact the case, then the boy might likely also be confused about the relationship with his father that would result from a marriage to his mother and the relationship that his parents would have with each other in the future. Children's perceptions of family relations must become confusing and disturbing when they attempt to think about the future and how their roles may change.

Children at slightly older ages, who have developed an understanding of how a person can be in two or more role relations simultaneously (Watson, 1984) and how a person might grow up, get married, and yet continue in a loving relationship with the parents, may be able to resolve the confusions in family roles and alleviate their insecurities. For example, to understand the true nature of mother-father-child triads is to realize that although the parents share an exclusive marital relation denied to the child, they also maintain a loving relation with the child that need not be threatened by their relation to each other. Also, when the child grows to adulthood and develops other social relations in his or her life, these need not destroy the ongoing relations with the parents. Such are the possibilities and the beauty of simultaneous role relations. Therefore, children's social-cognitive understanding of relationships with others and the sophistication of their conceptions of family roles may indeed be major factors in their perceptions of family structures and in the attendant emotions that accompany desires and threats to their sense of security in their relations.

Of course, other factors may also influence these family conflicts. Freud may have been partially correct in attributing one cause of the putative Oedipal conflict to changing sexual desires and the resolution of the conflict to the child's identification with the same-sex parent. The way in which parents show affection and also punishment to a child can influence the strength and nuances of this conflict. Also, the competition experienced with siblings and between children and parents for attention can be another influential factor. Nevertheless, we hypothesized that the child's own developing constructions of the structures of family role relations are the major factor in eliciting, first, confusion and differential preferences for parents and, later, resolution of the confusion and conflict. Regardless of individual family differences, we think all children go through a sensitive period between about four and six years of age in which they are forced to reexamine and renegotiate their relationships with their parents. And this renegotiation can temporarily place strain on the family—on the parents as well as the children.

In assessing this social-cognitive explanation of an Oedipal conflict, it must first be determined if Oedipal behaviors and feelings in children are normal and if they occur in a majority of older preschool-age children. To our knowledge, no systematic assessment of the prevalence of Oedipal behaviors in normal children in Western societies has been accomplished. The extant research comes mainly from case studies in which the Oedipus complex is already accepted as a given and is simply invoked to explain observations (for example, Conway, 1973; Galenson and Roiphe, 1980; Sachs, 1977). Therefore, the first objective of the present research was to assess the prevalence of some Oedipal behaviors in normal preschool children to determine if there is, in fact, a common increase in preference for the opposite-sex parent and antagonism for the same-sex parent at about four years of age and a subsequent decrease at about six years of age.

If Oedipal phenomena are indeed present in the behavior of most preschool children, then a second objective was to assess whether the social-cognitive explanation of the phenomena, introduced above, can be substantiated empirically. Fischer and Watson (1983) proposed the social-cognitive explanation that has been outlined here, but they did not empirically test it. The hypothesized relation between children's developing representations of family roles (as well as other social-cognitive concepts) and Oedipal behaviors is summarized below.

Before the Oedipal Conflict

This alternative explanation argues that children two to three years of age do not show Oedipal behaviors because they do not yet understand gender relations (for example, that males consistently marry females) and complementary role relations (that is, social roles in which one role is defined in terms of a complementary role). For example, a young child cannot conceive of a wife role in terms of a necessary husband-wife relation and instead concentrates on specific behaviors associated with wives. However, these children possess qualities that are precursors to the Oedipal conflict. Pre-Oedipal children are able to represent features of their environments that are frightening to them. In addition, because of their inability to coordinate mentally the actions of two people, they do not understand how one person can come to understand what another person is thinking simply by observing his or her behavior in a given context. For example, if a child yawns and rubs her eyes, the parent can infer that the child is sleepy, but the child may not be able to understand how the parent combined clues to make such an inference (see Gopnik and Graf, 1988). Thus, without seeing how parents can make these inferences, children are led to develop a belief in the omniscience of their parents. By the conclusion of this period, children have typically developed just enough understanding and confusion regarding their relationships to their parents to fall, head first, into an Oedipal conflict.

Oedipal Conflict

At about four years of age, children begin to understand social roles in terms of the complementary relations between them, not just in terms of specific behaviors (Watson and Amgott-Kwan, 1983; Watson and Fischer, 1980). For example, now a child realizes that one cannot be a wife without having a husband. With the development of gender constancy (Kohlberg, 1966; Liben and Signorella, 1987; Marcus and Overton, 1978), children also see male and female roles as complementary and constant. Since they are of one gender, they may be led to believe that they deserve the affection specifically of the opposite-sex parent, and they will focus more on their affectionate relation to that parent than to the same-sex parent. Moreover, because of a lack of understanding of multiple role intersections (that is, that one person can occupy several roles simultaneously), children may not realize that they can love each parent while their parents continue to love each other. In other words, children may not see how their parents can be both parents to them and spouses to each other and maintain both relationships simultaneously. In addition, children understand that by getting older they will become adults and may fill the roles of parents and spouses, but they do not yet understand the relativity of age, that as they age their parents will also. Thus, many children believe that they can catch up with their parents and step into one of their roles by marrying the opposite-sex parent.

An understanding of social role relations, age relations, and gender conservation leads children to think about their ability to fit into various family relations, including those of husband and wife and mother and father. However, children's inability to simultaneously coordinate all of these features leads to conflicts in their thinking about family roles (Fischer, 1980; Kuczaj and Lederberg, 1977; Marcus and Overton, 1978). Simply put, children get glimpses of the role relations that are possible for them, yet they get confused when they think that they can literally step into relationships already existing between their parents. Of course, these role confusions can exist for other relations as well, but children's relationships with their parents seem to be of prime importance to most children raised in nuclear families. Children's focus on family relations is likely due to their attachment to parents and need for the security and affection parents provide (as was illustrated in the anecdote provided at the beginning of this chapter).

Another source of confusion is that at the same time children are led to consider the exclusive attention of the opposite-sex parent, they may continue to believe that parents are omniscient, and thus that the same-sex parent is in each case aware of the child's interests. This belief may cause children to feel fearful of and negative toward the same-sex parent, and they may have a difficult time distinguishing internal fantasies from external realities (see DiLalla and Watson, 1988; Flavell, Green, and Flavell, 1986).

Resolution of the Oedipal Conflict

According to this proposed explanation, at about six years of age, children are able to resolve Oedipal conflicts because they develop an understanding of role intersections and because they also learn to coordinate age, gender, and role relations. Thus, children can continue to be the children of their parents at the same time that the parents carry on spousal relations. The children understand that as they age so also do their parents so that they can never catch up. Thus, a girl realizes that it does not make sense to marry her father or try to compete with her mother. She also understands how a parent can guess what she is thinking without being omniscient and how she can hide her thoughts and feelings from her parents.

In summary, the major hypotheses are that (1) Oedipal behaviors exist and emerge at four years and decrease at about six years in normal preschool children and (2) changes in Oedipal behaviors correspond to changes in children's role understanding, increasing understanding of the relativity of age, and decreasing belief in parental omniscience.

Method

Subjects. Forty middle-class children and their parents completed the study. There were ten children (five boys and five girls) in each of four age groups, with mean ages of 3.1, 3.9, 5, and 6 years. All children came from intact, two-parent families, and none suffered from any known psychological or physical health problems.

Procedure and Scoring. We collected data from two sources: parents' reports and children's doll-play narratives. Two scorers, blind as to the hypotheses of the study, independently scored all of the measures.

For the parents' reports, the experimenter instructed parents to keep a tally each day of the number of affectionate behaviors (for example, the child saying "I love you" or giving the parent a hug) and the number of aggressive behaviors (for example, the child saying "I hate you" or hitting the parent) that the child demonstrated. The experimenter called each parent each evening for seven consecutive days and recorded the day's tally and any additional comments that the parents made and then summed the tallies for each parent for the entire week. Parents were asked not to compare tallies or to discuss their observations with each other. The value of this data source rests in the independent perceptions of the parents about behaviors that are collected over several days and that can only be interpreted in the context they occur. It would not be reasonable for outside experimenters to judge which behaviors were considered particularly affectionate or aggressive in a particular family relationship.

In scoring these reported behaviors, we were not so much interested in absolute numbers as in the ratio between behaviors that could be considered Oedipal (that is, affection shown to the opposite-sex parent divided by aggression shown to the opposite-sex parent, and similarly for the same-sex parent) and behaviors that could not be considered Oedipal or might even be considered "anti-Oedipal." For these ratio scores, a ratio greater than 1 suggested a predominance of Oedipal behaviors; a ratio equal to 1 suggested no preferential behavior; and a ratio less than 1 suggested a predominance of non-Oedipal behaviors.

We also computed a second set of scores involving the differences between (1) the affectionate behaviors reported by the opposite-sex parents and the affectionate behaviors reported by the same-sex parents and (2) the aggressive behaviors reported by the same-sex parents and the aggressive behaviors reported by the opposite-sex parents. A positive affection-difference score suggested a predominance of Oedipal behaviors, and a negative score suggested a predominance of non-Oedipal behaviors. The same was true for the aggression-difference scores.

There was an interscorer reliability of 100 percent agreement on the tallies and ratio and difference scores. As expected, because of the independent reports of parents about the differential responses of their children toward them, these four parent scores (two ratio scores and two difference scores) were not highly correlated. By using all four scores, we were able to gain an assessment of the convergent validity of the Oedipal observations.

The second data source, doll-play narratives, was used to derive four different measures. Each child was brought by the mother to a playroom, and the mother sat behind the child and did not get involved as the experimenter acted out doll-play scenarios with the child. Doll-play tasks have been found to allow children to express their representations of themselves and others and their concern for conflicts and preferences, while maintaining some personal distance from the stories (see Bretherton, Ridgeway, and Cassidy, in press).

First, to assess *role-level understanding*, a doll family, consisting of parent, grandparent, and son and daughter dolls, was used to help enact a series of five stories. Each story corresponded to a step in a sequence of role understanding previously described and tested by Watson and Amgott-Kwan (1983). In this procedure, the child is allowed to take a turn enacting each story. The child's enactment of each doll-play story and his or her answers to follow-up questions were scored as a pass or a failure for each step in the sequence. The role-level score was the highest step passed by the child. The five steps are as follows: (1) independent agent in which the child demonstrates that a person (doll) can act independently of another person's actions, (2) behavioral role in which the child demonstrates a family role in terms of typical behaviors associated with that role, (3) social role in which the child demonstrates the complementary nature of role relations, (4) shifting social roles in which the child demonstrates how a person can shift from being in one role to another, for example, from being a mother to being a grandmother, and (5) role intersection in which the child demonstrates that a person can be in at least two roles simultaneously, for example, both mother and grandmother or both mother and wife. There was an interscorer reliability of 97 percent agreement on the steps passed. This sequence has already been shown to be reliable and valid (Watson and Amgott-Kwan, 1983; Watson and Fischer, 1980).

Second, to assess children's *Oedipal preferences in stories*, another doll family was used to help enact five stories thought to represent typical Oedipal issues. This second Oedipal assessment was thought to be more important than the parental reports because it was constructed to elicit the child's personal feelings and preferences. Again, the experimenter began with a story stem, then had the child complete the story, and finished the session by asking follow-up questions. Each story was scored as a pass if the child demonstrated a prototypical Oedipal completion and answered the questions in a way showing Oedipal feelings and preferences. The five stories concerned (1) whether the child (doll) would prefer to be with the opposite-sex parent or the same-sex parent, (2) whether the child would express a desire to marry the opposite-sex parent rather than someone else, (3) whether the child would try to compete with the same-sex parent by making a cake for the opposite-sex parent, (4) whether the child would be angry with the same-sex parent for interfering when the child was spending time with the opposite-sex parent, and (5) whether the child would obey each parent out of fear of punishment or out of affection.

The child's enactment of each story and answers to follow-up questions were scored either as a predominantly Oedipal response or as a non-Oedipal response. The Oedipal story score was the total number (0 to 5) of stories scored as Oedipal. There was an interscorer reliability of 90 percent agreement on the stories showing Oedipal responses. Interitem correlations resulted in a Cronbach alpha of .78, indicating a moderate level of internal consistency, considering the diversity of the stories.

Third, to assess *understanding of age relativity*, the experimenter asked the child a series of eight questions about the doll family, specifically, about the relative ages of the family members and how the relative ages would change or remain constant over time. This was a first step in assessing children's understanding of how age intervals remain constant over time. The age relativity score was the number of questions the child answered that demonstrated an understanding of constant age relativity. Interscorer reliability was 94 percent agreement for the answers on this measure. The Kuder-Richardson (KR20) reliability coefficient for these eight items was .80, indicating an adequate level of internal consistency.

Fourth, to assess a *belief in parental omniscience*, the experimenter used the doll family to enact two more stories and have the child complete them and answer follow-up questions. These two stories concerned whether the parents of the child doll could know what the child had done in private and what the child was thinking and how the parents might know this information. Each story was scored as a pass if the child demonstrated nonbelief in parental omniscience and gave other explanations for the parents' knowledge. Interscorer reliability for this measure was 94 percent agreement on the steps passed. In addition, almost equal numbers of children passed each of the two items, thus indicating no order of difficulty in the items.

Results

Two-way analyses of variance, using age (four levels) and gender (two levels) as independent factors were completed for all measures (see Table 1 for means and standard deviations). Newman-Keuls post hoc analyses were computed to assess differences between age groups ($p < .05$). Correlations were also completed between all variables.

Emergence and Decline of Oedipal Behaviors. The first hypothesis that Oedipal behaviors exist and emerge at four years of age and decrease at about six years was supported, with one amendment to the hypothesis. The initial decline in Oedipal behaviors was found to occur at five years rather than at six years of age (see Table 1). First, Oedipal story scores were significantly correlated with parent report scores (see Tables 2 and 3), indicating a degree of convergent validity in the assessments of Oedipal behaviors, in spite of the fact that these measures tapped different

Table 1. Children's Mean Responses
to Oedipal Tasks, by Gender and Age

Variable	Gender	Age (in years)			
		3	4	5	6
Mother ratio[a]	Males	1.40 (.81)	3.27 (2.31)	1.77 (.52)	1.80 (1.26)
	Females	0.86 (.57)	2.33 (3.20)	0.92 (.47)	1.18 (.25)
Father ratio[a]	Males	0.72 (.20)	2.43 (2.24)	1.26 (.83)	0.71 (.28)
	Females	2.50 (1.12)	4.07 (2.28)	2.30 (.67)	1.40 (.65)
Affection difference[b]	Males	0.80 (1.30)	2.00 (2.12)	0.80 (.84)	1.60 (2.07)
	Females	-0.40 (1.67)	1.60 (2.07)	-0.20 (1.30)	-0.40 (1.82)
Aggression difference[b]	Males	-0.60 (1.67)	2.80 (1.48)	0.20 (1.30)	-0.80 (1.79)
	Females	1.60 (2.07)	2.60 (2.70)	2.00 (1.58)	1.20 (1.64)
Story score[c]	(Both)	1.50 (.53)	3.70 (.67)	1.40 (1.17)	0.50 (.71)
Role level[d]	(Both)	2.00 (.67)	2.90 (.74)	3.70 (.95)	4.70 (.48)
Age relativity[e]	(Both)	5.10 (2.08)	6.10 (1.20)	6.70 (.95)	7.50 (.71)
Omniscience[f]	(Both)	0.40 (.52)	0.50 (.53)	1.80 (.42)	2.00 (.00)

Note: Standard deviations of means in parentheses.
[a] The higher the ratio, the greater the number of Oedipal behaviors versus non-Oedipal behaviors.
[b] Positive score signifies more Oedipal behaviors than non-Oedipal behaviors; negative score signifies the opposite.
[c] Range = 0-5; score signifies number of stories with Oedipal answers.
[d] Range = 0-5; score signifies highest step shown.
[e] Range = 0-8; score signifies number of answers showing an understanding of age relativity.
[f] Range = 0-2; score signifies number of stories in which a belief in parental omniscience was not shown.

behaviors and feelings and one set came from parents' reports and the other from children's representations.

For mother ratio scores, a main age effect approached significance $(F[3,32] = 2.33, p < .09)$, with ratio scores (Oedipal behaviors) peaking at four years. A main gender effect also approached significance, with boys showing higher ratio scores than found with girls $(F[1,32] = 3.07, p < .09)$. As might be expected, mothers reported more Oedipal behaviors for their sons than for their daughters.

For father ratio scores, there was a main age effect $(F[3,32] = 6.25, p < .01)$, with significant age differences between three and four and four and five years of age. There was also a main gender effect, with girls showing higher ratios than found with boys $(F[1,32] = 9.85, p < .005)$.

Complementary to the mothers' reports, fathers reported more Oedipal behaviors for their daughters than for their sons.

For affection-difference scores, there was only a main gender effect, with boys showing higher difference scores (more Oedipal affection) than found with girls ($F[1,32] = 5.10$, $p < .05$).

For aggression-difference scores, there was a main age effect ($F[3,32] = 3.61$, $p < .05$), with significant age differences between three and four, four and five, and five and six years of age. There was also a main gender effect, with girls showing higher difference scores than boys ($F[1,32] = 5.87$, $p < .05$). There were no age × gender interactions in any of these measures.

For Oedipal story scores, there was a main age effect ($F[3,32] = 28.33$, $p < .0001$), with significant age differences between three and four, four and five, and five and six years of age. There were no gender differences.

Because the pattern of Oedipal behaviors showed a curvilinear relation with age, all correlations were computed twice, once for three- and four-year-olds (see Table 2) and once for four-, five-, and six-year-olds (see Table 3). In this way, Oedipal behaviors were treated as part of two linear relations, increasing from three to four years and decreasing from four to six years of age. As can be seen in Tables 2 and 3, both parent scores and Oedipal story scores correlated with age, reflecting a rise in Oedipal behaviors at four years and a subsequent decline at five and six years of age.

Role Concept Development. The second hypothesis, that changes in Oedipal behaviors are related to changes in the three social-cognitive measures assessed, was supported. First, with the child's highest attained role-level as the dependent variable, a main age effect was found ($F[3,32] = 23.51$, $p < .0001$), with significant differences found between the mean role levels for children at each age (see Table 1).

Again, due to the curvilinear development of Oedipal behaviors, role level was correlated with Oedipal behaviors shown first at three and four years of age and again at four, five, and six years of age (see Tables 2 and 3). There was a positive correlation between role level and story scores at three and four years and a negative correlation with both parent scores and story scores at four to six years of age. As predicted, as role level increased, Oedipal behaviors increased from three to four years and then decreased from four to six years.

If changes in role understanding are indeed prerequisite to changes in Oedipal behaviors, then there should be a match between specific role levels and the presence or absence of Oedipal behaviors, regardless of the child's age. Evidence for such a match was found, but not for all of the children in the study. Of those children who reached only independent agents or behavioral roles as their highest role-levels, 25 percent (three out of twelve) showed Oedipal story scores of 3 or greater. Of those children who reached social roles as their highest level, and thus were

Table 2. Intercorrelations of Oedipal Story-Completion Scores and Parent Report Scores for Three- and Four-Year-Olds

Variables	Mother Ratio	Father Ratio	Affection	Aggression	Story	Role	Relativity	Omniscience
Father ratio	-.07							
Affection difference	.50ᵃ	.13						
Aggression difference	.62ᵇ	.38	.24					
Story score	.36	.46ᵃ	.21	.50ᵃ				
Role level	.08	.25	-.08	.09	.58ᵇ			
Age relativity	.06	.67ᵇ	.22	.29	.16	.21		
Omniscience	.15	.13	-.19	.10	.38	.37	-.09	
Age	.43	.46ᵃ	.41	.48ᵃ	.89ᶜ	.57ᵇ	.30	.10

Note: N = 20
ᵃ *p* < .05
ᵇ *p* < .01
ᶜ *p* < .001

Table 3. Intercorrelations of Oedipal Story-Completion Scores and Parent Report Scores for Four-, Five-, and Six-Year-Olds

Variables	Mother Ratio	Father Ratio	Affection	Aggression	Story	Role	Relativity	Omniscience
Father ratio	-.11							
Affection difference	.40[a]	.19						
Aggression difference	.49[b]	.45[a]	-.02					
Story score	.37[a]	.47[b]	.25	.48[b]				
Role level	-.35	-.37[a]	-.54[b]	-.40[a]	-.56[b]			
Age relativity	-.25	.15	-.15	-.15	-.45[a]	.55[b]		
Omniscience	-.24	-.49[b]	-.50[b]	-.37[a]	-.59[c]	.65[c]	.41[a]	
Age	-.22	-.58[c]	-.27	-.50[b]	-.82[c]	.72[c]	.53[b]	.81[c]

Note: $N = 30$
[a] $p < .05$
[b] $p < .01$
[c] $p < .001$

predicted to show Oedipal behaviors, 60 percent (six out of ten) showed Oedipal story scores of 3 or greater. Of those reaching shifting social roles as their highest level, 33 percent (three out of nine) showed story scores of 3 or greater. And of those reaching role intersections as their highest level, and thus not expected to show high Oedipal behaviors, 0 percent (none out of nine) showed story scores of 3 or greater. In other words, assuming now that Oedipal behaviors begin declining with shifting social roles rather than with role intersections, 75 percent (thirty out of forty) showed the predicted match of role level and Oedipal behaviors.

With children's understanding of the relativity of age as the dependent measure, there was a main age effect ($F[3,32] = 6.50$, $p < .005$), with significant differences found between three- and five-year-olds and four- and six-year-olds (see Table 1). There was a significant correlation of age relativity with the father ratio scores at three and four years (see Table 2) and with the Oedipal story scores at four to six years of age (see Table 3). Thus, as understanding of age relativity increased across age, there was some evidence for an associated decline in Oedipal behaviors and preferences, although the relation was not consistent across all measures.

With children's belief in parental omniscience as the dependent measure, there was also a main age effect ($F[3,32] = 14.53$, $p < .0001$), with a significant decrease in belief in parental omniscience found between four and five years of age (see Table 1). Also, belief in parental omniscience was significantly correlated with almost all the Oedipal measures at four to six years of age (see Table 2). Thus, as belief in parental omniscience decreased, Oedipal behaviors decreased also, particularly from four to five years (see Table 1).

Fairness Responses. An unexpected finding was a shift in children's explanations for choices in the hypothetical stories, namely, from responses demonstrating their strong parental preferences (for example, "Tommy wants to go with his mother because he loves her") to responses showing a fairness strategy of trying to keep preferences for parents balanced in the hypothetical families (for example, "Tommy went with Daddy last time, so it's only fair that he goes with Mommy this time"). No three-year-olds, two four-year-olds, three five-year-olds, and eight six-year-olds described their use of a fairness strategy at least once. The use of a fairness strategy correlated with age ($r[38] = .60$, $p < .001$), role level ($r[38] = .61$, $p < .001$), and Oedipal story score ($r[38] = -.44$, $p < .01$). This strategy may have taken the place of stronger, differential parent preferences as children got older.

Discussion

In summary, the results of the study suggest that there are behaviors that can be called Oedipal phenomena. These behaviors are observable by parents and converge with preferences and feelings that children express in play narratives accompanying projective story completions. The phenomena include an increased preference for the opposite-sex parent over the same-sex parent and more antagonism directed toward the same-sex parent than toward the opposite-sex parent, and they are significantly more frequent at four years of age than they are either earlier or later.

These findings are supported by comments made by a few of the parents of four-year-olds. One mother noted that her son had demanded, "Love me the most, Mommy, love just me the most." Another mother said, "My daughter always gives more attention to her dad." A father said of his daughter, "She told me that at bedtime I had to kiss her a hundred more times than I kiss her mother." And another father said that his daughter "came up to me and asked me to make her a bigger bed. She said that she needed more room for her dad to sleep with her." No parents of children at other ages made these kinds of comments.

Moreover, as Fischer and Watson (1983) hypothesized, these changes in Oedipal behaviors are related to changes in children's concepts of family role relations, belief in parental omniscience, and (to some extent) understanding of age relativity. Although these relations are clearly not causal in nature, and although precise matches have yet to be determined, they point to the strong possibility that children at about four years of age find themselves facing new ideas about their place in the family structure and about confusions surrounding their affections and preferences for parents. These confusions seem to lead to inner conflicts that can spill over to other members of the family, who may also react emotionally to the child's preferences and confusions. Although we did not assess possible emotional accompaniments of these Oedipal behaviors (such as feelings of guilt, shame, and insecurity), these feelings could likely be exacerbated by children's confusions about their present and future place in their families. Future research, particularly longitudinal studies, could clarify not only the synchrony of development in these different domains but also the possible accompanying emotional reactions of both children and parents.

Contrary to the original hypothesis, Oedipal behaviors declined significantly at five years of age. At about this age, when children typically develop an understanding that a person can shift from one role relation to another, they also begin to understand that multiple role relations exist and that both the child and the parents can participate in these multiple relations. In addition, children no longer show much belief in parental omniscience or in the possibility that one person can catch up with another person in age. Thus, this increased sophistication may allow the renegotiation of family relationships. It is noteworthy that, as we had hypothesized, most Freudians also have thought that the resolution of the Oedipal conflict occurs at about six years rather than five years of age.

The increased use of a fairness strategy for choosing parents in the stories, particularly at six years of age, also suggests that children become better over time at coordinating and comparing several family relations. Children's increasing use of fairness merits further investigation.

By six years, children are quite sophisticated in coordinating these various social-cognitive concepts and show very few differential parental preferences that could be called Oedipal. The crisis has passed.

Indeed, one implication of this optimistic explanation of the Oedipal crisis is that it is temporary, based on children's "growing pains," and, for normal children, will have little impact on permanent relationships (or on gender role development or superego development, as Freud believed), although children can use these experiences to learn more about social realities and the complexities of relationships. Children emerge from this sensitive period having tested their feelings and relationships. They have simply gone about the business of normal social and cognitive development.

In fact, the parents in the present study seemed to share an attitude that was in agreement with this optimistic explanation. Although we never mentioned the word "Oedipal" to the parents, many of them seemed to think that their four-year-olds were going through a phase in which they were trying to make sense of some complicated concepts that kept arising in the family (for example, "How is Grandma Dad's mother?"). The parents who commented on the Oedipal statements of their children, as cited above, considered these situations to be humorous and reasonable rather than unduly disturbing to either their children or to themselves.

Nevertheless, one prediction might be that parents who feed into this temporary crisis by threatening the security of their children (for example, through separation or through physical abuse) or who show extreme physical affection or sexual abuse may catch their children during a sensitive period of maximum vulnerability and thus may prevent them from using their increasing social-cognitive abilities to straighten out the confusions on their own (see Gill, 1987). Problem cases do require more research, in particular, studies matching clinical case histories with special problems that exacerbate minor crises and transform them into real Oedipal crises.

In addition, in light of this social-cognitive explanation, further research is likely to show that the emergence of family role confusions does not necessarily depend on the traditional family triad of mother, father, and child but may apply to less traditionally structured families as well. Children in single-parent families, for example, with or without siblings, should also exhibit confusions that will likely lead to concern for future roles and renegotiation of family relationships. And these redefinitions would be based primarily on the way children actively construct their own internal models of their families rather than on external crises.

References

Bretherton, I., Ridgeway, D., and Cassidy, J. "The Role of Internal Working Models in the Attachment Relationship: A Story Completion Task for 3-Year-Olds." In M. Greenberg, M. Cummings, and D. Cicchetti (eds.), *Attachment Beyond the Preschool Years.* Chicago: University of Chicago Press, in press.

Conway, A. "Oedipal Concerns of a Five-Year-Old Girl During Hospitalization." *Maternal-Child Nursing Journal,* 1973, *2,* 39–48.

DiLalla, L. F., and Watson, M. W. "Differentiation of Fantasy and Reality: Preschoolers' Reactions to Interruptions in Their Play." *Developmental Psychology,* 1988, *24,* 286–291.

Fischer, K. W. "A Theory of Cognitive Development: The Control and Construction of Hierarchies of Skills." *Psychological Review,* 1980, *87,* 477–531.

Fischer, K. W., and Watson, M. W. "Explaining the Oedipus Conflict." In K. W. Fischer (ed.), *Levels and Transitions in Children's Development.* New Directions for Child Development, no. 21. San Francisco: Jossey-Bass, 1983.

Flavell, J. H., Green, F. L., and Flavell, E. R. "Development of Knowledge About the Appearance-Reality Distinction." *Monographs of the Society for Research in Child Development,* 1986, *51* (1, serial no. 212).

Freud, S. "Analysis of a Phobia in a Five-Year-Old Boy. In *The Sexual Enlightenment of Children.* New York: Collier, 1963. (Originally published 1909.)

Freud, S. *New Introductory Lectures on Psychoanalysis.* New York: Norton, 1965. (Originally published 1933.)

Galenson, E., and Roiphe, H. "The Pre-Oedipal Development of the Boy." *Journal of the American Psychoanalytic Association,* 1980, *28,* 805–827.

Gill, H. S. "Effects of Oedipal Triumph Caused by Collapse or Death of the Rival Parent." *International Journal of Psychoanalysis,* 1987, *68,* 251–260.

Gopnik, A., and Graf, P. "Knowing How You Know: Young Children's Ability to Identify and Remember the Sources of Their Beliefs." *Child Development,* 1988, *59,* 1366–1371.

Kohlberg, L. "A Cognitive-Developmental Analysis of Children's Sex-Role Concepts and Attitudes." In E. E. Maccoby (ed.), *The Development of Sex Differences.* Stanford, Calif.: Stanford University Press, 1966.

Kuczaj, S. A., II, and Lederberg, A. R. "Height, Age, and Function: Differing Influences on Children's Comprehension of *Younger* and *Older.*" *Journal of Child Language,* 1977, *4,* 395–416.

Liben, L. S., and Signorella, M. L. (eds.). *Children's Gender Schemata.* New Directions for Child Development, no. 38. San Francisco: Jossey-Bass, 1987.

Malinowski, B. *Sex and Repression in Savage Society.* New York: Meridian, 1955. (Originally published 1927.)

Marcus, D. E., and Overton, W. F. "The Development of Cognitive Gender Constancy and Sex Role Preferences." *Child Development,* 1978, *49,* 434–444.

Pollock, G. H. "Oedipus Examined and Reconsidered: The Myth, the Developmental Stage, the Universal Theme, the Conflict, and the Complex." *Annual of Psychoanalysis,* 1986, *14,* 77–106.

Sachs, L. J. "Two Cases of Oedipal Conflict Beginning at Eighteen Months." *International Journal of Psychoanalysis,* 1977, *58,* 17–31.

Sears, R. R. *Survey of Objective Studies of Psychoanalytic Concepts.* New York: Social Science Research Council, 1942.

Spiro, M. E. *Oedipus in the Trobriands.* Chicago: University of Chicago Press, 1982.

Watson, M. W. "Development of Social Role Understanding." *Developmental Review,* 1984, *4,* 192–213.

Watson, M. W., and Amgott-Kwan, T. "Transitions in Children's Understanding of Parental Roles." *Developmental Psychology*, 1983, *19*, 659–666.

Watson, M. W., and Fischer, K. W. "Development of Social Roles in Elicited and Spontaneous Behavior During the Preschool Years." *Developmental Psychology*, 1980, *16*, 483–494.

Malcolm W. Watson is associate professor of psychology at Brandeis University.

Kenneth Getz is a graduate student in the Kellogg School at Northwestern University.

*The Bears' Picnic, a new test of preschoolers' representations
of self and family, was given to four-year-olds who had been
observed with their mothers at twenty months of age. Observed
maternal sensitivity and the affective quality of both partners
were related to the child's later valuing versus devaluing of self
and others.*

The Bears' Picnic:
Children's Representations of
Themselves and Their Families

Edward Mueller, Elizabeth Tingley

How do preschool children mentally represent their parents, siblings,
and families? Some researchers seek the answer directly, asking children
to describe their images or beliefs about their parents. In this research,
we have used fantasy or story-telling material in an attempt to understand
children's core representations, both of their families and of themselves,
representations that we believe are outside the child's awareness and thus
not available for direct assessment.

Children seem to be unaware of many of their core beliefs about self
and other. Thus, we chose a technique involving specific stories depicted
in a doll-play scenario called the "Bears' Picnic" (henceforth BP). At
present the BP is only a research instrument; it is not yet a norm-refer-
enced test. The BP is an attempt to reveal both self-concept and other-
concept, aspects of the child's representational world that may play a
large role in a child's sense of self-identity and self-esteem.

The stories chosen stem from the interaction of three trends of
thought in modern psychology: cognitive, cultural, and developmental.
We consider each of these trends here and how they overlap and inter-
connect.

The authors acknowledge the assistance of professor emeritus Henry Weinberg in
contributing to the ideas in the introduction. We also acknowledge the support
of the John D. and Catherine T. MacArthur Foundation Network on the Transition from Infancy to Early Childhood.

Cognitive Bases of the BP

On the whole, modern developmental psychology, psychodynamic research, developmental psycholinguistics, attachment theory, and artificial intelligence oppose the view of a transparent consciousness that can be adequately understood using self-report measures of personality alone (Horowitz, 1979). In each of these fields of study, the concept of the schema has assumed a prominent theoretical role. As Horowitz (1985, p. 8) suggests,

> schemata summarize past experience into holistic, composite forms, thus allowing incoming information to be measured against the existing composite for "goodness of fit." In forming a conscious experience of thought, information from the internal composite may be used to fill out forms missing in the external stimulus information. While this may lead to rapid perception in some ways, it may also lead to patterned and recurrent errors in interpreting and responding to stimuli that are actually different from the schematic forms.

If schemata underlie all of our intellectual and linguistic efforts, as Piaget (1952) has claimed, are they not likely to underlie our interpersonal efforts also?

Schemata go by many names, for example, rules, operations, goals, "affective templates" (Fein, 1987). In this chapter, the schemata that we believe the BP uncovers are called "images" and "representations," in line with Sandler (1987, p. 63). He theorizes that the representational world

> might be compared to a stage set within a theater. The characters on the stage represent the child's various objects, as well as the child himself. Needless to say, the child is usually the hero of the piece. . . .
> . . . Whereas the characters on this stage correspond, in this model, to self- and object-*representations,* their particular form and expression at any one point in the play corresponds to self-and object-*images.*

This distinction between images and representations is central to how we analyze children's stories from the BP. Each story provides an image, a particular "scene" of the play where certain events are depicted. For example, in the first story, the main character bear (henceforth MC) may get stung by bees, while in the next story, he or she may trip and fall over a rock in the forest on the way to a picnic. While each story represents only a single image from the child's representational world, their similarity suggests that both images are compatible with a more general self-representation of the MC as "vulnerable." We can say that the actor was playing a vulnerable character. And just as Sandler sees that children place themselves as heroes of their plays, so we infer that the action of the MC is likely to involve self-representations, and that the depiction of other characters in the story involves "other-representations." The term "objects" is Sandler's term for what often amounts to the significant others in one's life, and so we label them "other-representations."

At the same time it is important not to construe the distinction between self- and other-representations in BP stories too rigidly. Recall that the characters of the play could never really "play their parts" without a good knowledge of the roles of all of their fellow characters. The same criterion holds for the representation of others by the self. They are also well understood by the self and thus are always present as potential roles for the self as well. This could be why helpless, abused children become abusive themselves in role playing, when they can at last reverse roles by virtue of having their own helpless babies.

Notice that in the above discussion we are describing cognitive schemata with the language of theater or drama. But if the schemata revealed by the BP have much to do with metaphors like the theater and play, then we are already interrelating cognitive bases and cultural ones, because dramaturgical language is usually associated with cultural, not cognitive, descriptions. So let us consider the cultural bases of the BP more directly.

Sociocultural Bases of the BP

Representations of the social world, including those of self, derive gradually from social participation. For example, by about ten months of age, children and their mothers share about seventeen social games (Camaioni and Laicardi, 1985), and most of these become generalized to peer relations by about eighteen months of age (Mueller, 1988). It may be easier to study the child's representations of games than those of self and other because the shared understanding of a game such as peek-a-boo is overtly enacted when the social game is performed. In contrast, representations of significant others may control behavior more in the absence of partners than in their presence, as Robertson (1953) found in studies of children's reactions to photographs of their mothers during continuing separations.

Still, there is no reason to think that meaningful representations of self and other are derived in different ways from these schemata for social games. Stern (1985) supports the view that core representations of self and other also have their bases in social participation. While the ability to form representations appears more and more to be pre-wired (see Stern, 1985), the meaningful understanding of self as good or bad, or of other as caring or rejecting, must await postnatal social participation.

In both the case of social games and self- and other-representations, meaning that was initially only in the mind of the significant other (because meaning, an inherently mental phenomenon, can exist only in minds, though it can be signaled through communication) gradually comes to be understood (that is, constructed through semantic representation) by the child. For example, from repeated interactions, the child may gradually form the following representations: "I am worthy and valuable; mother is admiring and gentle." It is this positive representation that in theory causes the child to form positive images of both self and other in imaginative acts of constructing BP stories.

It is important to note that the representations of self and other derivable from BP stories are always meaningful. Although the capacity to understand the world meaningfully is probably innate, and even though some emotional states may be understood meaningfully from birth onward (Campos and others, 1983), all *evaluative* meanings about self and other must be acquired after birth during times of shared understanding that we call "shared meanings" (Brenner and Mueller, 1982). To qualify as a specific shared-meaning game, both participants must clearly understand the whole meaning of routines like peek-a-boo with their complementary roles of "sudden appearance" and "positive affective acknowledgment." For toddlers this can only be evidenced through their actions, that is, by their actively playing both roles at different times. Yet, how did either participating toddler understand the peek-a-boo meaning in the first place? One possibility is that the meaning simply emerges from the interaction. However, given our premise that meaning itself exists only in the human mind, not in physical reality, this explanation is without foundation. The most common source of learned meaning deducible from our data on toddler-peer communication is generalizations from meanings acquired through earlier parent-child communication (Mueller, 1988). Thus, peek-a-boo, as a shared social routine, probably has its origins in the attachment relation, in attempts to keep visual contact with the original object of love and security. Through peek-a-boo routines, parents show their child that their physical reoccurrence is a more or less predictable event after disappearance and that they are in this sense trustworthy. This example shows how the attachment figure is the original cultural funnel or filter through which the culture's meanings are assimilated in however veridical or distorted a manner (Henry Weinberg, personal communication, 4 November 1989), a process that may explain how the family, especially the original attachment figure, has such extraordinary influence in the formation of the child's core sense of self and other. This parental scaffolding of meaning in interactive sequences is seen as the birthplace of a child's evaluative meanings about self and other (Hodapp and Goldfield, 1985).

All communication involves the transmission of multiple levels of meanings (Watzlawick, Beavin, and Jackson, 1967). While the specific content at the moment may be peek-a-boo, the more abstract content may be "you are a valuable child worthy of my time and attention." It is this more abstract message that may form the more or less continuous message, the higher-order meaning, extracted by the child from thousands of specific, shared-meaning games (Stern, 1985). As higher-order abstractions, influenced by the child's self-perception as well as by external input, these mental representations may never have appeared in quite their final form in actual interactions (see Strauss, 1979). In just this sense, then, they are "imaginative constructions" or fantasies. By fantasy we do not mean that such representations are experienced as unreal but only that they are purely beliefs; they are not subject to reification, to being regarded as material things or as simple verbal labels.

These evaluative meanings are thus appropriately studied through story-telling or projective techniques, techniques aimed at tapping fantasy and imagination. In the BP, children do not have time to ponder their stories, to reflect on the stories told. Instead, they are faced with ambiguous situations and must just say whatever comes into their heads. This context is rather different, say, from that of the novelist with ample time to study the character of adult acquaintances and bring them into a novel. Because the BP stories are requested so immediately, we believe the imagination must appeal directly to the core schemata of self and other. This conceptual tie of the imagination to the representations of self and other is the theoretical assumption necessary to understanding the logic of the BP. One of our students, not understanding, or not accepting this assumption wrote, "I agree that the children are less aware that they are revealing anything about themselves [in the BP], but who is to say that they are revealing anything? The story could be entirely fantasy!" "Excellent," we reply, the more immediate the fantasy, the better, because the more likely is the story to derive from core representations of self and other. Fantasy does not come from a vacuum. While some stories may derive from yesterday's television show and are thus not spontaneous at all, most stories derive from the self, giving substance to the notion that "creativity has its roots in the personality."

Developmental Bases of the BP

In the prior section we noted that some representations of self and other were more "core" than others. Why should this be? If representations are a product of shared meanings, then as shared meanings about self and other change across a life span, so too should representations of self and other. The research of developmental psychology, especially attachment research (see Bretherton, 1987), suggests that the earliest relations in life seem to generate representations of self and others that attain a kind of fixity or crystallization. One might almost say that the first five or six years of life form a critical period for the formation of character, and that basic character normally shows little change thereafter (see Freud, 1916).

Various explanations for this development might be proposed. One is that the earliest representations are formed in a preverbal mode, and that once children switch to verbal operations it is hard to regress to the earlier mode of functioning to change what is there. Another explanation is simply Piaget's idea that all development stems from accommodations of existing schemata. For this reason, no matter how much we change in life, we are always growing from changes in the original template laid down in the first relationship, no matter how modified it may become over time.

This is why the family is of such extraordinary importance in the character formation of the child, an emphasis that is mimicked in the social contexts of the BP story stems. At the time the earliest template is forming, the key other in the child's life is the attachment figure. Because the child has no evaluative self to begin with, the attachment figure is powerful in assigning to the child representations of self and other from which the child has no buffer, no "preformed" self. In the American psychology literature, the security function of the attachment figure has been emphasized (Roopnarine, Cochran, and Mounts, 1988). But probably of equal or greater importance in the child's emotional health is the role of the attachment figure in forming the meaningful representations of self and other often called the "internal working model of self and other" (Bretherton, 1987). Secure versus insecure emotional states may be more a product of these representations than the reverse. That is, the child develops secure versus insecure emotional states because his or her initial representation of the attachment figure is one of being valued versus devalued.

Varieties of Family and Self Role Depiction in the BP

To further clarify the meaning of the BP stories, it is helpful to speak in terms of role relationships in the family. Assume that careful observational study of one father-son pair reveals that the father "devalues the child as shown through arbitrary punitiveness." The same study also shows that his son responds to paternal outbursts with "appeasing actions and helplessness." Now assume that this same child provides valid evidence for the above observations by telling a father-child study where the father bear acts punitively and the MC bear responds with appeasement and helplessness. Because the father's and the son's "roles" in the relationship are performed in the story, we must conclude that the child has represented not only his own role but also that of his father. Which role, then, characterizes the child? From the point of view of the representational world, the answer is both roles. From the perspective of role learning, we see then that no hard and fast line can be drawn between "self" and "other" material in the BP story. For this reason important family material about member devaluation should be studied regardless of whether it was attributed in the story to the MC bear or to others in the family.

One way to circumvent this whole problem of "what to attribute to whom" is to analyze the BP stories for material about the characteristics of family relationships in general. While no such analysis could be completed here, we take the first step of suggesting which important dimensions of family functioning (such as the dominance dimension just discussed) are represented in the material of BP stories.

Value of the BP for Interventions

The BP is appropriate for use with children at ages four to six. We have suggested that such children are still young enough to be in the process of forming their core representations of family and self. Thus, when the BP detects negative representations of self and other, there still may be time for effective family intervention prior to the crystallization of such representations. This is the potential clinical importance of the BP, since accurate diagnosis without the ability to intervene effectively is usually fruitless.

Method

Subjects. The BP was administered to twenty-seven middle-class, four-year-old children, thirteen boys and fourteen girls, who were part of a larger sample gathered principally for the longitudinal study of temperament and its sequelae conducted at Harvard University (Kagan, Reznick, and Gibbons, 1989). All of these subjects had been videotaped at twenty months of age as they interacted with their mothers in a structured play session. In this session mothers and children were first asked to engage in free play in a toy-rich environment. Then, most toys were put away and they were asked to play with the toys located in four boxes numbered 1 to 4. The boxes contained a ball, a blanket for peek-a-boo, crayons and paper for drawing, and a picture book, respectively.

Description of the BP. The BP consisted of six story stems. Story stems are incomplete stories that must be finished by the child. The examiner presents a set of toy bears including a mother, a father, a boy, and a girl, and props including a tree, a wagon, a picnic blanket, a ball, a pot of honey, and a pot of food. The child is handed the child bear that corresponds to the child's sex and is told that "we are going to make up some stories about this bear." This bear is called "your special bear" to foster the child's identification with this bear. The child usually accepts this definition of the action, and as a result most of the stories involve this bear serving as the main character or MC.

There is a warm-up story in the test, where the examiner conveys to the child an openness to fantasy and playfulness. In the warm-up play, the examiner makes some suggestions about what the "your bear" likes to do, such as running and doing somersaults, and then gives the first warm-up story that the child is asked to complete. The examiner says the following: "Suddenly, your bear looks up in the tree and sees a big pot full of delicious honey. Bears love honey. She/he really wants the honey! What happens next?" The goal here is to get the child to complete the story of the presented situation. If the child says "I don't know" or "you tell me," the examiner presses the child to take over the story by asking again, "what do you suppose your bear will do to try and get that honey?" or asking the child how the bear feels about the honey. Above all, the examiner attempts to get the child engaged in play and focused on the task of making up stories.

After this phase, the child is given the test story stems and is asked each time "what happens next?" The test has been revised several times, but for the sample reported here there were six vignettes. The story stems and the images of the self and important social others that the stories were designed to elicit are presented in Table 1. Not all these story stems are original to this test; some emerged from research cooperation among those participating in the MacArthur Network on the Transition from Infancy to Early Childhood (see, for example, Bretherton, Prentiss, and Ridgeway, this volume).

What unites the stories here is our commitment to the importance of assessing the child's images of his or her family: mother, father, and siblings. Every story in this set concerns the self in relation to the family or to the issue of separation from the family.

Procedure. The BP was administered in each case during a home visit made by one female examiner who was blind to the ratings of earlier mother-child interactions. Each session was videotaped, and all family members except the child were asked to leave the room during the testing. In addition, at age twenty months, the children and mothers were video-taped during both a free-play and a semi-structured-play procedure. These sessions were analyzed for the quality of the mother-child relations, and the relationship between these ratings and the self-/other-evaluations made by children in the BP stories was examined. Finally the stories were subjected to a content analysis to discern common themes and typical responses.

With respect to the content of the code for the BP, this study examined the quality of a child's relation to his or her mother at twenty months of age as related to three outcome variables—fantasy failure, valuing, and devaluing, each coded from the story-telling material on the

BP at four years of age. A case method also was used to compare the BP stories of two children at opposite ends of these outcome variables. In addition, a new code about quality of family relationships was derived from the responses to the BP stories, but an independent sample of stories was not available for verifying the code's utility.

The BP stories were first scored for the three markers of fantasy failure, positive valuing of self or other, and negative valuing of self or other.

At the heart of this scoring system is the notion that the tendency of the child in fantasy to make positive or negative statements about the characters reveals the child's inner model or template of self and other. The criteria utilized for each marker and examples of each are shown in Table 2.

Table 1. Content and Familial Purpose of Each Bears' Picnic Story

Story	Story Stem	Familial Purpose
1.	One day the bear family went for a picnic; bears love picnics. The mommy and daddy bear are over here busy setting up the picnic. Your bear decides to play with the wagon. Can you make your bear pull the wagon? Then the brother/sister bear comes over and says, "can I play too?" What happens next?	Sibling image: social cooperation versus competition
2.	The children bears are still playing with the wagon when suddenly the wheel falls off. Whoops. Daddy bear comes over and says, "what's going on over here?" What happens next?	Paternal image as supportive or punitive
3.	Mommy bear is picking blueberries from the bushes and she is *very* busy. Your bear wants to play ball with her. What happens next?	Maternal image as supportive, rejecting, or punitive
4.	Your bear and sister/brother bear go for a long walk in the woods, way, way over here. Suddenly sister/brother bear trips over a rock and hurts her/his leg and can't get up. What happens next?	Self-image: competence, resourcefulness, or helplessness
5.	Now the bears are ready for their picnic. The bears are very hungry and they start gobbling down the bear chow. But your bear is so hungry that she/he knocks over the bowl and all the bear chow spills right on the picnic basket. What happens next?	Parental understanding: forgiveness versus punitiveness and hostility
6a.	Now the bears are ready to leave. Mama bear starts to fold up the blanket but it's too hard for her to do it by herself. What happens next?	Family image of mutual help and cooperation
6b.	Now its time for your bear to go to school. What happens next?	Separation; self-resourcefulness; parental support; image of the larger world as safe or unsafe

Table 2. Markers of Socioemotional Factors in the Bears' Picnic Stories

Category	Criteria
Fantasy failure	Negative: Child does not produce associations to story stem for fifteen seconds or more after interviewer says "what happens next?" or child either refuses to or simply does not complete the vignette. Even if child begins with "I don't know" or "you tell me," failure is not scored unless child persists beyond fifteen seconds with such statements.
Valuing: MC values family member or MC is valued by a family member	Positive: When MC expresses concern for, help toward, liking of, or is otherwise altruistically inclined toward one or more of the family figures. Also scored positive when other figures are portrayed as helping, caring, or nurturing in relation to MC.
Devaluing: MC devalues family member or MC is devalued by a family member	Negative: When MC expresses hostility or selfish behavior toward one of the family figures, or instances where one of these figures is the victim of accidents and other violent or unpleasant events. Also scored negative when other figures are portrayed as hostile, unjustly or arbitrarily punitive, rejecting, or hurtful in relation to MC.

Negative valuing of self/other in each story vignette was scored with a minus. Positive valuing of self and other in each vignette was scored with a plus. Each marker was scored only once per vignette. For each child, the total number of pluses and minuses in each of these categories was computed. We have already discussed the rationale for combining the valuing/devaluing both from and toward the main character.

Interrater agreement was computed with an intraclass correlation coefficient using three coders and a sample of ten complete protocols of the BP. The resulting coefficients were .79 for total pluses and .89 for total minuses. Following Cicchetti and Sparrow's (1982) guidelines, these results were in the "excellent" range.

Second, the stories were analyzed for their family content. This was done by reviewing all of the videotapes to locate common themes and issues portrayed in the stories. One set of themes emerged that described the child's portrayal of the emotional tone of family life, for example, anger, blame, affection, reassurance, and reasonableness. Another set of themes included the description of relationships within the family as cooperative or conflictual, engaged or unengaged, and equal or dominant. Common themes and typical examples are later described.

In addition, two individual cases were examined, one where the child told a set of positive stories, and one where the child made many statements devaluing of self and other. The independent ratings of the quality of the mother-child interaction at twenty months of age, together with characterizations of these two sets of stories, are later presented to demonstrate possible relations between quality of mother-child relation at twenty months and represented sense of self and other at four years of age.

Mother-Child Interaction at Twenty Months. The play sessions at twenty months were analyzed with a 7-point rating scale on dimensions of mother-child interaction: 7 corresponded to excellent, or a definite strength in the interaction; 6 corresponded to above-average behavior; 5 indicated behavior slightly above average; 4 indicated average, neither positive nor negative, behavior; 3 corresponded to somewhat below-average behavior; 2 indicated below-average behavior; and 1 reflected the lowest rating, a definite weakness in the interactional pattern. All scoring was done on a comparative basis, that is, across mother-child pairs.

Four dimensions of interaction were examined: maternal sensitivity, sharing of control, child affect, and maternal affect. These dimensions were chosen for three reasons. The first was their salience, especially maternal sensitivity, in other work on the early mother-child relationship (for example, Ainsworth, Blehar, Waters, and Wall, 1978). The second was their appropriateness to a developmental understanding of the toddler's growing need for autonomy within relationships, thus the sharing-of-control dimension (for example, Erikson, 1963). The third was simply empirical validity, that is, review of the videotapes validated that these four dimensions of interaction were in fact observable in this play session.

There were five separate play episodes within each play session, and each episode was rated on each dimension using the 7-point scale. Then a composite score for each dyad on each dimension was derived by averaging across all play episodes. Behavior such as maternal initiation of activity during a pause by the child or maternal elaboration of child actions was rated high on maternal sensitivity, whereas behavior such as maternal persistence with an activity in the face of clear opposition by the child was rated low on maternal sensitivity. Instances where both partners took the lead and followed the other at different points in the interaction were rated high on sharing of control. Interactions where one partner, either mother or child, was in control throughout and the other was compliant or where both strived for control and did not succeed were rated low on sharing of control. Affect was rated positive when happiness, enthusiasm, pleasure, or joy was clearly expressed, whereas affect was rated negative when at least one partner seemed unhappy, depressed, angry, or hostile.

Three raters examined ten of the play sessions, and interobserver agreement was calculated using interclass correlations. Their agreement within a step for these scales varied from .77 to .97.

Methods of Data Analysis. Across-time correlations were calculated between the ratings of mother-child relationship at twenty months and the marker codes on the BP at four years of age. Common themes in the stories were extracted along with typical examples of each.

Results

Mother-Toddler Interaction and Self- Versus Other Valuing in the BP. The twelve Pearson correlation coefficients of the ratings of mother-child interaction at twenty months (that is, sensitivity, sharing of control, child affect, and maternal affect) with the BP codes at four years (that is, fantasy failure and self-/other valuing and devaluing) were computed. While five correlations approached significance, only two correlations actually were significant: Maternal sensitivity at twenty months was negatively related to the frequency of devaluing of self/other in story content ($r = -.46$, $p = .02$). In other words, the higher the ratings of maternal sensitivity, the lower the number of devaluing remarks in the BP stories. And conversely, the lower the ratings of maternal sensitivity, the higher the number of devaluing remarks in BP stories. The other significant relation applied only to boys. Namely, maternal affect at twenty months was negatively correlated with the amount of devaluing of self and other ($r = -.56$, $p < .05$). In other words, when mothers at twenty months were rated as using mostly positive affect with their boys, the boys were less likely to devalue self or other in fantasy play at four years of age. And conversely, when mothers were rated as employing mostly negative affect, their boys were more likely to devalue self and other at four years.

Three other correlations approached significance. For girls, maternal sensitivity was negatively correlated with the fantasy failure total ($r = -.48$, $p < .08$). This indicates an inverse relationship between maternal responsiveness to child cues or signals at twenty months and girls' ability to produce fantasy during the BP. For boys, maternal sensitivity was negatively correlated with the amount of devaluing of self and other ($r = -.54$, $p < .06$), and child affect was also negatively correlated with amount of devaluing of self and other ($r = -.53$, $p < .06$). When mothers were less sensitive to boys in toddlerhood, boys' stories were more likely to contain negative events or statements about the bear characters. Or, when mothers were more sensitive to boys in toddlerhood, few negative attributions and events occurred in their stories at four years of age. Similarly, the results suggest that when boys' affect was highly positive at twenty months, fewer devaluations of self and other were produced in play, and vice versa.

Two other correlations for the boys were above $r = .40$ but not significant ($p < .15$). These two correlations are worth noting, given the small sample size, since they involve the relationships between maternal affect and valuing of self and other in play, and between sharing of control and devaluing of self and other. Sharing of control and total instances of devaluing of self and other in fantasy play were negatively correlated ($r = -.43$, $p < .14$). Maternal affect and valuing of self and other were positively correlated ($r = .44$, $p < .13$).

Perceptions of Family Relationships in the BP. Beyond the basic representation of self and family in positive or negative ways, the stories children produced on the BP contained many complex characterizations of family relationships. Many diverse and subtle views of the quality of the relationships between family members, in the quality or emotional tone of family life, and in the capacities of the self to manage social or emotional conflicts were expressed in the BP fantasy play. In what follows, the views of these aspects of the family found in the BP are described, giving common responses and specific examples from the stories created by the children.

Three dimensions of family relationships were portrayed in the BP: engaged or unengaged, equal or dominant, and cooperative or conflictual. Consider first the engaged versus unengaged dimension. Some children, despite potentially conflictual themes, were able to portray family members as engaged with each other, even though the relations were negative. Other children told all six stories without depicting any contact at all between one or another family member. For example, in the broken wheel story, one response was for the MC to tell the father bear that the wheel fell off and then the father bear either fixed the wheel or responded accusingly or punitively toward the MC. In either case, interaction had occurred. However, another response was for the MC to ignore the father bear and to fix the wheel himself; some children even stepped out of the story narrator role and fixed the wheel "themselves." Again no contact between the MC and father bear was enacted. Other instances of unengaged relations occurred in stories where there was active avoidance between family members. For example, in one story, the child had the mother bear turn her back when the father bear called. In another case, when the sibling bear fell down, the MC hid in the wagon and then flew away never to return. In these cases lack of contact resulted not from omission but from direct avoidance by the characters. Thus, one dimension of self and other presented in the BP stories was the amount of engagement between family members.

The second dimension of family relationships was the equality or dominance between individuals. When actions were mutually defined by the characters and when characters shared rewards and problems evenly, the child seemed to be representing relations of equality. Conversely, when one character told another what to do and how to do it or when one character was in charge of what others received, the child seemed to be representing relations of dominance. It is interesting that one relation often portrayed as dominant was the sibling relation. The child frequently characterized the MC as bigger and more capable than the sibling, with the MC telling the sibling what to do. Instances of dominant relations between the MC and the parent bears included the MC getting hit, being told to stay outside in the cold and rain, and being prohibited from touching the food. Occasionally the relation between the parent bears showed dominance, with the father bear acting as the "boss" of the mother bear. In other cases the parents were equal partners in solving problems. At times the whole family seemed in an equal and balanced relation. For example, one child said, "Everybody gets a turn eating."

The third dimension of relationships that four-year-old children portrayed was conflict or cooperation between individuals. Stories of conflict included those where the characters were aggressive toward each other, thwarted each other's wishes, or disagreed with each other. In an instance of disagreement between characters, one child had the mother bear refute the statements of the father bear about his own impending death, saying "He's faking it." Cooperation refers to instances where the characters acted together toward a common goal, or adjusted themselves to the needs and wishes of others. For example, one child said the following in response to the sibling story stem: "The little sister got in the wagon, and the brother pulled her. The sister said, 'You're going too fast,' and the brother said, 'Okay' and then he went slower." The picnic clean-up story, in particular, often elicited complete family cooperation, with all members volunteering to help the mother fold up the picnic blanket.

In addition to these three dimensions of relations, children can portray many varieties of what might be called the emotional tone or quality of family life. The stories reported here included both implicit and explicit references to family life as angry, reassuring, rational, aggressive, punitive, helping, affectionate, and gratifying. Some children told stories that were fairly consistent in emotional tone throughout. For instance, one child explicitly described at least one character as angry in the first four stories. In other cases, children attributed a variety of emotions and qualities to the bear family. In one set of stories the MC both kicked the sibling and received a hug from the father bear.

The aggression depicted included kicking the sibling, breaking "mommy and daddy's favorite trees," kicking over the honey, throwing the ball at the mother, kicking over the father, and dumping over the wagon. Among the punitive actions were the following: "He'd [father bear] smack the children," "No soup for you [MC]," and "She's [mother bear] gonna wrap him up in the picnic blanket and keep him [MC] outside in the cold and rain." Affection between the bears, for example, hugs and kisses, was also present in the stories. And characters were shown offering reassurance to each other. To the spilled-food story stem, one child said, "She'd [mother bear] say that's all right." In another case, the MC said to the sibling after a fall, "You're okay, little bear."

Another quality of interaction represented in play was an attitude of reasonableness or rationality between characters. That is, the bears provided helpful explanations to each other for events and behaviors, including details of cause and effect. For example, some children explained that the mother bear, though presently busy picking blueberries, could play later. One child, in the broken wagon story, had the MC say to the father bear, "We went over a rock." In another case, the child said about the spilled soup, "No cover and it spilled. He didn't watch where he was going, but he told the truth, and the mother bear didn't punish him." In these instances some children showed that they valued rationales in the discipline and interactions of family members.

Children also showed family members as gratifying the wishes of others. One mother bear, when the food spilled, went to get better food, "raspberries and blueberries," for the children bears. When the MC expressed a wish for the honey pot or for a playing companion, others in the family gave what was desired. Finally, another quality of interaction often present in the stories was helpfulness. Several of the story stems put the MC in situations that could be resolved easily with assistance. The parent bears were shown quite frequently giving whatever aid was needed. The MC was also shown asking for help in several stories.

The ability of the MC to manage the numerous demands presented in the story stems also varied a good deal across stories and story tellers. The MC sometimes was portrayed as very competent and resourceful, for example, fixing the wagon wheel, cooking more food when the soup was spilled, giving the hurt sibling a Band-Aid or running to get a parent bear, getting to or from school on his or her own, and helping the mother bear fold the blanket. In one case the child had the MC say, "I fold good." In other cases, the MC portrayed both self and family as helpless, such as when a child bear, unable to reach the honey, whined and said that no family member was tall enough to get it for her.

Also, the MC was often presented as being vulnerable to unexpected, scary, or dangerous events. Monsters, dark tunnels, deep holes, wagon crashes, and getting lost all figured in events depicted in the stories. In some cases, the MC coped well with these events, emerging as the hero. For example, one child told a story where the sibling was in a wagon accident and the MC told the sibling how to get out of the wreckage and find her way home. At other times, the story ended with the MC or others seemingly still hurt or in danger.

Thus, in these stories, children painted multidimensional pictures of the bear family. They portrayed relationships as unengaged or engaged, dominant or equal, conflictual or cooperative; family life as angry, punitive, aggressive, rational, reassuring, gratifying, affectionate, and helping; and the self as competent, helpless, or vulnerable.

From these examples we have concluded that the BP can be an effective tool for eliciting children's representations of their families. To date there has been no systematic analysis of the relations between the dimensions expressed in stories and prior ratings of mother-child interaction. However, given the correspondence between the ratings of the quality of mother-child relations and the valuing/devaluing of self/other statements in the BP stories, we expect that these qualitative dimensions of depicted family life can be shown to relate systematically to actual family interaction and its representations in the BP. For example, children who have experienced insensitive and controlling caretaking during the toddler period might be more likely to act out stories showing the family and self in conflict. Or, again with the early experience of unresponsive caretaking, the child might portray family relations in the BP as unengaged.

Two Cases. Summaries of the stories told by two children, along with descriptions of the interactions between these two children at twenty months and their respective mothers, are now presented here. These two cases clarify the meaning of the valuing/devaluing codes of the BP and their relation to the earlier mother-child relationship.

In the first case, the child was responsive to the examiner's lead in beginning the stories, but he was also very creative and positive in his solutions to the events given in the story stems. His stories were as follows: The MC first had his sister play with him on the wagon and then the bear family took a rest together. When the wheel broke, the father bear fixed it with help from the mother bear. When asked by the MC, the mother bear readily agreed to stop picking blueberries to play ball. They threw the ball back and forth very playfully. After the MC spilled the food, the father bear got water to clean it up. The sister bear flew back to the parent bears when she got hurt. She then told the mother bear what happened. The MC next asked the father bear how to help the hurt sister and the father bear brought them all home. The mother bear flew to school with the MC, but he came home on his own and played with sister bear.

In the second case, a girl could not adapt to the story line given by the examiner. Her stories were difficult to understand because much of each story remained in the child's mind and was not made clear to the listener. She also smiled broadly as one terrible event after another occurred. Her stories were as follows: The MC didn't let the brother play and was happy as the sibling cried to the mother. The mother bear and sibling bear then left together without the MC. When the wheel fell off the wagon, the child provided no solution, and then the father bear died. When the food was spilled on the picnic blanket, the child looked anxious and searched for another story line. As the examiner insisted on the theme, the father bear turned into a scary monster, and the children had to "get out." When the monster changed back into the father, he was still angry. At this point, the mother told the children to run from the father bear. Later, the mother bear went off by herself and got lost.

There are clear contrasts between these two four-year-olds' stories, the first portraying a positive view of the family as helpful and supportive, and the other presenting a much more negative view of the family as scary and punitive. And, as indicated above, the amount of valuing of self and other expressed in the first stories corresponded with high ratings of maternal sensitivity, sharing of control, child affect, and maternal affect at twenty months. Throughout the free play and the semi-structured play, the mother in the first case was quite flexible in her responses to her son. For example, in the free play, the child changed his focus several times and the mother followed his topic. At one point the child stopped for a moment to sit in a chair and said "Hi" to his mother, seemingly asking for emotional contact. The mother shifted to a calm, quiet tone and looked and smiled at the child. In the semi-structured play, this mother allowed the child to participate in opening each activity box and followed his lead and interest in deciding when to present a new activity. In the last activity, the mother tried several strategies to get her son involved in book reading, but the child started to climb after the ball. Laughing, the mother allowed the activity to return to ball play. Throughout the play both mother and child exhibited appropriately varied affect. Both often expressed excitement and pleasure in the play, and their affective responses were matched with one another.

Conversely, in the second case, elevated amounts of devaluing corresponded to low ratings of maternal sensitivity, sharing of control, child affect, and maternal affect at twenty months. Throughout the free play and the semi-structured play, the mother's pace was faster than that of the child. At many moments, just as the child began to focus on an activity, the mother changed it. For example, as the child started to explore the jack-in-the-box, the mother said, "Want me to do it?" and took it from the child's hand; the girl in turn looked bewildered by this. In addition, the mother often physically moved her daughter without any noticeable verbal or nonverbal warning and positioned her to complete actions the mother defined. In one instance the mother physically sat the child down and spread her legs for "roll the ball," all occurring at a time when the child was otherwise engaged. During the book reading, the mother tried to hold the child in her lap even when the child protested strongly. During semi-structured play, any off-task activity by the child was treated by the mother as a distraction; she used a disparaging tone when responding to these off-task actions. During one three-minute sequence, the mother either talked to the child while she had her back turned or else ignored the child completely. Overall, the mother's affect had a frantic quality. In these case examples, then, the relations between the quality of interaction at twenty months and the quality of stories the children told at age four can be seen quite concretely. Specifically, insensitive and controlling early caretaking was related to later story material high in conflict, domination, and danger, whereas early sensitive, responsive, and affectively positive caretaking was related to stories of cooperation, harmony, and helpfulness in the bear family.

Conclusion

This chapter shows the promises of story-telling procedures in understanding children's representations of their families and themselves. The central result was that maternal sensitivity to the child in play interaction at twenty months was related to the child's valuing or devaluing of self and others at four years of age. The small sample size did not allow us to analyze this result separately for the devaluing of self versus a sense of devaluing by other family members; however, a rationale was given for why these two forms of valuing and devaluing may be interconnected. Other findings suggested that expressed affect (happy/sad) by both mother and child may be significantly related to the representation of the family at age four.

To further illustrate these results, summaries of the actual BP stories of two children were presented. In the first, the quality of the actual relationship had been rated positively at age twenty months, whereas, in the second, the relationship had received low ratings for maternal sensitivity, sharing of control, and maternal affect. These results were used to illustrate the general hypothesis that the child's negative or positive representation of self and family is significantly influenced by the quality of early social experiences in the family.

Beyond these findings, the chapter developed a set of categories devised from BP stories for the socioemotional analysis of children's representations of general family characteristics. The main categories derived from a review of the actual BP data collected were engaged versus unengaged, equal versus dominant, and cooperative versus conflictual. No systematic analysis was attempted here between these three dimensions and the quality of mother-child relations at twenty months. As with the valuing/devaluing, self/other code, it is likely that the qualities of family life portrayed in the BP reveal the child's inner representations of significant relationships with family members. The relation between early experience and these dimensions is an important topic for future research.

References

Ainsworth, M. D., Blehar, M., Waters, E., and Wall, S. *Patterns of Attachment.* Hillsdale, N.J.: Erlbaum, 1978.

Brenner, J., and Mueller, E. "Shared Meaning in Boy Toddlers' Peer Relations." *Child Development*, 1982, *53*, 380-391.

Bretherton, I. "New Perspectives on Attachment Relations: Security, Communication, and Internal Working Models." In J. Osofsky (ed.), *Handbook of Infant Development.* New York: Wiley, 1987.

Camaioni, L., and Laicardi, C. "Early Social Games and the Acquisition of Language." *British Journal of Developmental Psychology*, 1985, *3*, 31-39.

Campos, J. J., Barrett, K. C., Lamb, M. E., Goldsmith, H. H., and Stenberg, C. "Socioemotional Development." In M. M. Haith and J. J. Campos (eds.), *Handbook of Child Psychology.* Vol. 2. New York: Wiley, 1983.

Cicchetti, D. V., and Sparrow, S. S. "The Behavior Inventory for Rating Development." *Proceedings of the American Statistical Association, Social Sciences Section.* Cincinnati, Ohio: American Statistical Association, 1982.

Erikson, E. *Childhood and Society.* New York: Norton, 1963. (Originally published 1950.)

Fein, G. G. "Pretend Play and Consciousness." In D. Gorlitz and J. Wohlwill (eds.), *Curiosity, Imagination and Play: On the Development of Spontaneous Cognitive and Motivational Processes.* Hillsdale, N.J.: Erlbaum, 1987.

Freud, S. "Some Character Types Met with in Psychoanalytic Work." In J. Strachey (ed.), *The Standard Edition of the Complete Works of Sigmund Freud.* Vol. 14. London: Hogarth, 1916.

Hodapp, R. M., and Goldfield, E. C. "Self- and Other Regulation During the Infancy Period." *Developmental Review*, 1985, *5*, 121-136.

Horowitz, M. J. *States of Mind.* New York: Plenum, 1979.

Horowitz, M. J. "Program on Conscious and Unconscious Mental Processes." Unpublished manuscript, John D. and Catherine T. MacArthur Foundation, Chicago, 1985.

Kagan, J., Reznick, J. S., and Gibbons, J. "Inhibited and Uninhibited Types of Children." *Child Development*, 1989, *60*, 838-845.

Mueller, E. "Toddlers' Peer Relations: Shared Meaning and Semantics." In W. Damon (ed.), *Child Development Today and Tomorrow.* San Francisco: Jossey-Bass, 1988.

Piaget, J. *The Origins of Intelligence in Children.* New York: International Universities Press, 1952.

Robertson, J. "Some Responses of Young Children to Loss of Maternal Care." *Nursing Care*, 1953, *49*, 382-386.

Roopnarine, J. L., Cochran, D., and Mounts, N. "Traditional Psychological Theories and Socialization During Middle and Early Childhood." In T. D. Yawkey and J. E. Johnson (eds.), *Integrative Processes and Socialization: Early to Middle Childhood.* Hillsdale, N.J.: Erlbaum, 1988.

Sandler, J. *From Safety to Superego.* New York: Guilford, 1987.

Stern, D. N. *The Interpersonal World of the Infant.* New York: Basic Books, 1985.

Strauss, M. S. "Abstraction of Prototypical Information by Adults and Ten-Month-Old Infants." *Journal of Experimental Psychology: Human Learning and Memory*, 1979, *5*, 618-632.

Watzlawick, P., Beavin, J., and Jackson, D. *Pragmatics of Human Communication.* New York: Norton, 1967.

Edward Mueller, associate professor, and Elizabeth Tingley, graduate student, are both developmental psychologists at Boston University.

A semi-projective, picture-based, separation anxiety test, scored for attachment quality and emotional openness, was related to observed attachment status.

Five-Year-Olds' Representations of Separation from Parents: Responses from the Perspective of Self and Other

Nancy M. Slough, Mark T. Greenberg

Looking at the attachment relationship to parents from the child's perspective can provide valuable insights regarding the development of children's views of self and others. This chapter describes a method for exploring children's thoughts and feelings about their attachment relationships via an indirect examination of their cognitive-affective representations. These representational responses are shown to relate to their observed attachment behavior with their mothers.

A variety of closely related developmental theories (Bowlby, 1973, 1980, 1982; Winnicott, 1965; Stern, 1986) describe the critical importance of parental responsiveness to their infant's needs. These theories also

This research was supported by U.S. Department of Health and Human Services, Maternal and Child Health Services research grant #MCJ 530487. We are grateful to the mothers and children who participated in the study and to doctors Keith A. Crnic and Heather Carmichael-Olson without whose assistance this study would not have been possible. We also appreciate the assistance provided by Dr. Mary Main, Anitra DeMoss, and Diane Majerus with the scoring of our videotapes. Thanks also to Dr. Molly Reid for her helpful suggestions for this manuscript, and particularly to Michelle Goyette for her invaluable contribution to the SAT coding system.

hypothesize that the mental images a child forms of the self and others are constructed from the quality of these early child-caregiver exchanges. Attachment theorist John Bowlby (1973) has termed these images "internal working models" and has hypothesized that the working models an individual develops in early childhood of the self and parent are complementary. For example, children who feel secure in their attachment relationship have a representation of their parent as accessible and responsive to their needs; they therefore feel safe from harm and danger. Furthermore, along with the children's model of a loving and responsive mother, children are likely to develop perceptions of themselves as persons who feel confident and deserving of such love. This positive self-image can be exhibited in a variety of ways, including the child's ability to trust in, love, and feel close to others. In contrast, children with insecure attachments to their parents may perceive them as inaccessible, unresponsive, or even rejecting. These children may not feel confident that they are loved or their individual working models of the self may reflect an image of someone who feels unworthy of being loved. In turn, insecure children may have difficulty in forming trusting relationships with others.

Of course, there are generally a number of people in the child's life who significantly affect how the child perceives others. Brothers and sisters and nonprimary caretakers all contribute to the child's perception and internal model of how relationships work. However, the primary attachment figure, generally the mother or father, is believed to be of greatest importance in how the child's working model of self develops.

In the first and second year the quality of the attachment relationship is usually assessed by examining infants' behavior prior to, during, and after a separation from a caregiver. Recently, however, investigators have begun to study the nature of attachment relationships in older preschoolers by capitalizing on their growing verbal abilities, that is, they have also begun to query children about their cognitive-affective representations or working models of attachment relationships (for example, Main, Kaplan, and Cassidy, 1985; Bretherton, Ridgeway, and Cassidy, in press).

One difficulty in assessing such affect-laden representations lies in determining the veracity of the respondent's answers. Bowlby (1980) proposed that distortion of the internal working model occurs through the intrapsychic process of defensive exclusion. Defensive exclusion is likely to occur when the individual excludes from conscious processing those images or representations that are too anxiety provoking. Despite the individual's lack of conscious awareness, these images may have a significant impact on the person's behavior, particularly when under stress. Thus, the child's responses to questions about relationships cannot necessarily be construed as direct reflections of actual events; they instead may be representations of how those events have been processed. Hence, Ainsworth (in press) has suggested that assessment of the preschooler's internal working model of self and others should explore how defensive exclusion is manifested. For example, children who manifest an avoidance pattern upon reunion with their parents would also be expected to avoid (that is, defensively exclude) attachment-related material in other contexts (Cassidy and Kobak, 1988).

A variety of methods have been used to elicit children's thoughts about attachment-related issues. Main, Kaplan, and Cassidy (1985) utilized an adaptation of the Separation Anxiety Test (Klagsbrun and Bowlby, 1976) to assess six-year-olds' reflections on separations from their parents. This test is a semi-projective measure consisting of six photographs of mild (for example, going to bed) and severe (for example, parents leaving for vacation) separations between young children and their parents. Main and her colleagues have reported highly significant relationships between children's attachment security to mother (but not to father), assessed at both twelve months and six years of age, and their "emotional openness" in responding to the Separation Anxiety Test. The scale of emotional openness (Kaplan, 1984; Main, Kaplan, and Cassidy, 1985) is a rating of children's ability to freely discuss feelings of vulnerability when asked questions about how the child in the separation picture feels. Children who are able to express their feelings about the separations with relative ease, that is, without losing control or with minimal resistance, are given the highest rating of 9 and are considered emotionally open. Those children receiving ratings of 1, or emotionally closed, are unable to express their feelings, deny having any feelings, or lose behavioral control in response to the pictures. It is likely that at least some children who received low ratings on this scale were defensively excluding from awareness anxiety-related material regarding their attachments.

In the present study, we investigated the different ways in which five-year-old children manifest or represent their internal working models of attachment relations using a revised version of the Separation Anxiety Test (henceforth SAT). In previous administrations of this test (Klagsbrun and Bowlby, 1976; Kaplan, 1984), children were shown a picture of an impending separation between parent and child and were only asked questions that referred to the child in the picture, that is, how the child felt and how the child would cope with the separation. In our pilot sample we incorporated alternate probes to see whether children might provide different answers when asked how *they* (the interviewees) would feel in the same situation. The pilot data revealed that some children did indeed alter their answers between probes. Asking the questions about the self and a peer provided an opportunity for the children to present the self as more self-reliant or more emotionally vulnerable than the peer. We felt that this information would provide further insight about the structure of children's internal working models. For example, if the children were able to express themselves more easily under the guise of the child in the picture, this may indicate that some material regarding the self was being defensively excluded. In this chapter we focus on individual differences in how children discuss the feelings and expected actions of the self and another child during the SAT. Since this information is derived from stimuli concerning parent-child interactions, we believe the data provide a means of assessing children's perceptions of their closest family relationships.

In addition, we assessed the children's attachment relationships to their mothers through observations of separation-reunion sequences in the laboratory. By investigating the relationship between an observational measure of attachment quality and children's responses to the SAT, we attempted to determine which set of SAT responses (for self or other child) was most concordant with observed attachment behavior.

Participants and Procedure

This study involved sixty five-year-olds and their mothers who were participants in the Mother-Infant Project, a longitudinal study of premature and full-term infants and their mothers. From the original sample of fifty-two premature and fifty-three full-term subjects (see Crnic and others, 1983, for a complete description of the original sample), complete attachment data at age five were collected on twenty-six premature and thirty-four full-term dyads. No differences between the two groups were found on any measure assessing attachment at age five. Overall, the total sample was largely white and middle class, with half of the children being male, half being first-born, and the mean age of the children being five years and one month.

All of the procedures in which each child participated took place in a room equipped with one-way mirrors to allow observation and videotaping of the session. Two female research assistants conducted the two-and-one-half-hour sessions, which involved a number of structured and unstructured situations designed to explore various components of the mother-child relationship. Of interest here are the SAT and reunion procedures.

During each session, the mother was asked to leave the room for two separation-reunion sequences. The first, a "short" separation (three minutes in duration), followed approximately forty minutes of other activities. The mother was instructed when to leave the room but could explain her leaving to her child however she chose. The child was left alone in the room with a plastic horse and a newly acquired gift (a kaleidoscope). Mothers were not given instructions on how to behave upon reunion and no particular emphasis was placed on the matter.

Following the first reunion, the mother and child had a short break that was followed by a "long" separation (approximately one-and-one-half hours). During this separation the mother was interviewed in a separate room while the child was given a variety of developmental tests and the SAT. After completing the testing the child remained in the room (one to two minutes) while the examiner went to get the child's mother. As in the previous reunion, mothers reunited with their children in their natural manner.

Measures

The SAT. The SAT, a semi-projective test, is an adaptation of Hansburg's (1972) original measure, which was designed to assess the way in which adolescents (ages eleven to seventeen) respond to separations from, or loss of, their parents. Klagsbrun and Bowlby (1976) modified Hansburg's test so that it could be used with younger children (ages four to seven). They reduced the number of pictures from twelve to six, eliminated some of the more disturbing depictions (for example, father and child standing by mother's coffin, mother being taken away in an ambulance), and substituted photographs (still shots from movies) for Hansburg's ink drawings. Each photograph was designed, with the aid of a caption, to provide a clear situational context and yet remain ambiguous in emotional expression. Drawings based on these photographs were used in the previously discussed study of six-year-olds (Main, Kaplan, and Cassidy, 1985).

For the current study, new photographs were taken to solve some of the problems found with the Klagsbrun-Bowlby photographs (primarily the lack of consistency between the sets of girl and boy pictures). The new photographs retain the same situational contexts as the originals, but a number of modifications were made: (1) showing mother *and* father in all but two of the scenes (in which only the mother is pictured); (2) using the same setting, parents, and props for the boy and girl pictures; (3) updating the photographs with more modern clothes and hairstyles; and (4) showing only the children's profiles or backs of their heads to help maintain ambiguity in facial expressions. The photographs depict the following situations (in order of administration): (1) parents go out for the evening, leaving child at home; (2) parents go away for the weekend, leaving child with aunt and uncle; (3) child's first day at school, moment of parting from mother; (4) parents go away for two weeks; prior to their departure they give child a present; (5) park scene, parents tell child to run off and play alone for awhile because they want some time alone together to talk; and (6) mother tucks child in bed and leaves room.

Klagsbrun and Bowlby (following Hansburg) considered three of these separation situations to be mild and easily handled by children (scenes 1, 5, and 6); the other three they considered severe and more difficult for children to handle (scenes 2, 3, and 4). Our expectations differed somewhat from Klagsbrun and Bowlby. We felt that the picture of the parents leaving the child, apparently alone, to go out for the evening was severe, and that the picture of separation on the first day of school was relatively mild, since most of the children in our study had already attended preschool or daycare programs.

Before administering the SAT, the examiner and child interacted in a variety of situations so that a comfortable rapport was established. As each photograph was presented, the scene was explained to the child and followed by a series of questions: "How does the little girl (boy) feel?" "Why does she (he) feel that way?" and "What's the little girl (boy) going to do?" If the child did not answer one of the questions or if the response was unclear, the examiner would encourage the child to "tell me more" or "just tell me what you think, there are no right or wrong answers." After completing the set of questions about the child in the picture, the examiner then asked the child being interviewed how she or he would feel and behave if she or he were the child in the picture.

Theory-Based Scoring for the SAT. Scoring indices and ratings for the SAT were created as an overall measure of the child's working model of attachment to parents. They assess differences in the children's thoughts about their abilities to cope with mild and severe separations. Specifically, we predicted that if a child had formed a working model of a responsive and accessible caregiver, the child should express confidence and feelings of well-being in the context of the easier separations. But when confronted with a more difficult (anxiety-arousing) parental separation, a securely attached child should be able to express any concerns, fears, or feelings of sadness about the separation since it is expected that the caregiver will also be responsive to those concerns. In contrast, an insecure child might respond in a variety of ways (for example, claim self-reliance, even in the difficult separations; be totally unable to talk about the separations; discuss the separations illogically or with significant hostility).

The scoring indices and ratings were designed to reflect three dimensions of the children's answers: expression of vulnerability/need, that is, *attachment*, expression of *self-reliance*, and *avoidance* of verbal expression. Scoring of the SAT was done in three stages:

Major Categories of Response. Responses to each picture were first classified into one of the five major categories of SAT indices: attachment, self-reliant, attachment/self-reliant, avoidant, or additional (see Exhibit 1). Categorizations were based on the valence of the feeling and the justification for the feeling. Attachment answers reflect sadness or anger about the parents leaving. Self-reliant answers include feelings of well-being because the child in the picture is comfortable with the parents leaving

Exhibit 1. Main Categories and Subcategories of the Separation Anxiety Test Scoring Indices with Example Responses

Example format: The child's answers to the questions, "How would you feel?" "Why?" and "What would you do?"

Attachment
1. Typical attachment: <feel?> "He'd be sad, <why?> because the parents are leaving, <do?> he'd play"
2. HI attachment: "I'd be sad, because my parents were going out, I'd stay with a babysitter"
3. LO attachment: "Sad, 'cuz I like to feel sad, play"
4. Attachment/retribution: "Sad, because I can't be around 'em, run off home and stay there and cry on bed 'til they get there"
5. Attachment/increase access to parents: "Sad, because my parents are leaving, go find them"
6. Atypical attachment: "Happy, 'cuz I would go with them, just say, 'No, I'm going' "

Self-Reliant
7. Typical self-reliant: "Happy, because I like to be alone sometimes, sit and play with toys"
8. HI self-reliant: "Happy, because somebody's with her, play with them"
9. LO self-reliant: "Good, just would, go outside and play hide and seek"
10. Atypical self-reliant: "Sad, because he'd have to live with the aunt and uncle, he would stay with a babysitter"

Attachment/Self-Reliant
11. Typical attachment/self-reliant: "Happy and sad, because there is a present but her parents are leaving, play and make dinner"
12. HI attachment/self-reliant: "Happy and would find a babysitter, but kinda sad because they left, he'd play in his room while the babysitter is there"
13. LO attachment/self-reliant: "Feel? happy and mad, why? because lots of reasons, do? play"
14. Attachment/self-reliant/image of parents: "There's no babysitter? Sometimes they feel happy, or sad, or OK, if there's a babysitter just go in his room and pretend mom and dad are there"
15. Attachment/self-reliant/increase access to parents: "Happy that she has someone with her, sneak out a window. . . follow Mom and Dad"

Avoidant
16. Avoidant: "I don't know . . . I don't know"
17. Avoidant/confused: "Sad and furious, 'cuz a cat was in my house, I don't know"
Also, subcategories 3, 6, 9, 10, and 13

Exhibit 1. *(continued)*

Additional

18. Anxious: "Nervous, because she's never been to school before, math and stuff"
19. Anxious/increase access to parents: "Scared, because she thinks the parents are leaving, follow 'em"
20. Atypical: "Happy, because his mom and dad are going away, he has a dog, play with his dog"
21. Bizzare: "Happy, 'cuz her mom's leaving for the rest of her life," (no response to "What would you do?")

or focuses on an aspect of the situation other than the separation. The attachment/self-reliant classification reflects components of both categories. Avoidant answers reflect the interviewed child's inability or reluctance to respond to a picture (for example, one-word answers with no elaboration, total silence, or an insistence on not knowing what the child in the picture feels or what that child would do). The additional category includes answers that indicate anxiety or those with content that deviates from the norm or indicates emotional disturbance.

Subcategory Scoring. As also indicated in Exhibit 1, each response was placed into its appropriate subcategory, based primarily on the coping response in answer to the question, "What would the child (you) do?" Typical answers are those in which the child copes by performing an appropriate activity such as playing or watching television. HI and LO refer to particular types of responses and are not ratings per se. For example, a HI coping response involves finding someone else to be with when the parents leave (for example, "he'd get a babysitter"). Other subcategories reflect a *specific* coping style. For example, subcategory 14, attachment/self-reliant/image of parents, includes answers in which the child thought or dreamed about the parents, wrote them a letter, or called them on the phone. (Further details about subcategory assignments are in the coding manual, available upon request from the authors.) Interrater reliability for categorization of the response across the six pictures was 88 percent for those pertaining to the other child and 90 percent for those pertaining to self.

Summary Ratings of the SAT Indices. To convert the SAT indices into summary ratings, a 4-point *attachment* rating scale (4 = high to 1 = low) was applied to the responses to each of the three *severe* separation pictures: parents leaving for the evening, leaving the child with the aunt and uncle, and parents leaving for two weeks. Similarly, a 4-point *self-reliance* scale was used to rate the responses given to the three *mild* separation pictures: child's first day at school; park scene; mother tucks child in bed. The 3-point *avoidance* rating scale (3 = high to 1 = low) was applied to the responses to all six pictures.

For the attachment, self-reliance, and avoidance dimensions, two summary scores (one for the child's own responses and one for the hypothetical child) were then computed by adding ratings across the appropriate stories. The attachment and self-reliant scores are independent of each other, since they are based on different pictures. The avoidance scale is only partially independent of the other two. Although a high avoidance score assigned to a response precludes it from receiving a high rating on either of the other two scales, a low rating on either of the attachment or self-reliant scales does not necessarily require a high rating on avoidance.

Scale of Emotional Openness. This 9-point scale (9 = high to 1 = low) rates the child's ability to express feelings of vulnerability and yet still maintain his or her self-control. As described by Kaplan (1984), children receiving high scores can verbalize feelings of sadness, fear, loneliness, or anger and offer reasons for their feelings (for example, "I would be angry because my parents wouldn't take me"). They are also able to offer ways of coping with separations without demonstrating avoidance and disorganization or being overly self-reliant. Children who earn middle scores show some imbalance between their abilities to disclose feelings (self-exposure) and self-control (self-containment). The lowest scores are given to those children who manifest behaviors such as an inability to discuss their feelings, extreme denial of feelings, or out-of-control behavior. Children were assigned two emotional openness scores, one for their own responses to the six separations and one for responses attributed to the child in the picture.

In the present study, interrater agreement for the scale of emotional openness, when referring to the child in the picture, was 50 percent exact agreement and 74 percent agreement within one scale-point; when referring to the self, the corresponding figures were 50 percent and 71 percent. Agreement between coders across responses concerning self was 50 percent exact and 71 percent within one scale-point.

Scoring of Attachment Reunions. Quality of the child's attachment was scored for both the short and long separations-reunions. For the short separations-reunions (long separations-reunions are discussed later), attachment quality was assessed using the scoring system developed by Main and Cassidy (1985, 1988) for six-year-olds. Each child was scored on two rating scales: a 9-point security-of-attachment scale (9 = very secure to 1 = very insecure) and a 7-point avoidance scale (7 = very strong avoidance to 1 = no avoidance).

Coders of the reunions were trained by one of the authors (Greenberg), who was trained by Main's staff at the University of California, Berkeley. Disagreements were first discussed and, if not settled, were refereed by a third coder (Greenberg). Coder agreements for the short separations-reunions on the security and avoidance scales were $r = .74$ and $r = .70$, respectively.

Results and Discussion

The children's responses to the SAT pictures were quite varied. Some of the children were interested in the pictures and asked questions about who the people were, if the examiner knew the child in the picture, and so forth. In contrast, a few children almost refused to look at the pictures after the first two or three were presented. Some children became very fidgety when a severe separation picture was shown and yet seemed to relax when looking at a mild scene. Other children discussed the separations enthusiastically when talking about the pictured children but became silent when discussing themselves. In short, it was clear that the picture stimuli were emotionally meaningful for these five-year-olds.

In this section, we begin by examining the data on the relationships obtaining between the children's responses for self and their responses for the hypothetical other child on the SAT. We then look at how the children's responses concerning the self versus the other relate to the child-mother attachment relationship as measured by data from the short separations-reunions. Next, we explore which children provided different responses for themselves versus the hypothetical others on the components of the SAT summary scores. Finally, some implications, derived from comparisons of the data on self versus other child are discussed.

Throughout the tables presented in this section, results are reported for both the other (the child's rating when asked about the pictured child) and the self (the child's rating when asked about himself or herself) on the attachment, self-reliance, and avoidance summary scores.

Relationship Between Self and Other Measures. The intercorrelations among the SAT responses are presented in Table 1. As shown, the relationships between like variables scored for both the other child and the self in the SAT summary scores are fairly high (ranging from $r = .41$ between other and self on self-reliance to .58 between other and self on avoidance), but these correlations appear to be indicating somewhat different aspects of the children's internal representations. In contrast, the correlation between the SAT emotional openness scores for other and self is extremely high ($r = .91$), indicating that the two variables cannot be considered different measures. However, this high correlation may be an artifact of how the SAT was administered. Because each child interviewee was asked questions about the other child and then about the self for each picture, the answers for the pictured child and for the self were interspersed during the interview sessions. Thus, differentiating emotional openness scores for self and other from responses across the pictures proved difficult except in those cases where the interviewee was consistently quite open when responding in reference to the self but quite closed when responding in reference to the pictured child, or vice versa.

Table 1. Correlations Among Separation Anxiety Test (SAT) Responses, by Category

SAT Measures	Emotional Openness		Avoidance		Self-Reliance		Attachment
	Self	Other	Self	Other	Self	Other	Self
Attachment							
Other	.49[b]	.49[b]	-.43[b]	-.51[b]	.19	.22	.54[b]
Self	.66[b]	.53[b]	-.73[b]	-.44[b]	.33[a]	.08	
Self-Reliance							
Other	.07	.09	-.16	-.41[b]	.41[b]		
Self	.33[b]	.39[b]	-.62[b]	-.34[a]			
Avoidance							
Other	-.54[b]	-.55[b]	.58[b]				
Self	-.67[b]	-.65[b]					
Emotional Openness							
Other	.91[b]						

[a] $p < .01$

[b] $p < .001$

Relationship Between Separation-Reunion Behavior and SAT Responses. The relationship between the short-separation-reunion responses and the responses on the SAT are shown in Table 2. Overall, higher correlations were found between the ratings of attachment (security versus avoidance) in the short separations-reunions and the scores for self on the SAT than between the ratings of attachment and the scores for the other child. This suggests that, at least for some of the children, the ways in which they discuss (or avoiding discussing) themselves in the context of separations is more closely related to their attachment status than is their discussion of hypothetical peers.

Of the three SAT summary score components, attachment, self-reliance, and avoidance, the avoidance measure shows the strongest relationship to the short-separation-reunion measures. This result appears to reflect the kind of consistency in response across different contexts discussed by Cassidy and Kobak (1988). The more avoidant the child was during the SAT, the more insecure he or she was during the separation-reunion sequence. The fairly strong relationship between the short-separation-reunion measures and emotional openness also supports this interpretation. In contrast, the rather weak relationship between the short-separation-reunion variables and the SAT attachment summary scores suggests that a five-year-old's ability to expose and justify feelings of sadness, regret, or anger, at least in the context of severe separations, may be only slightly related to attachment status.

**Table 2. Correlations Between Separation Anxiety Test
(SAT) and Separation-Reunion Responses, by Category**

SAT Measures	Short-Separation Security	Short-Separation Avoidance
Attachment		
Other	.22[a]	-.17
Self	.27[a]	-.37[b]
Self-Reliance		
Other	.16	-.23[a]
Self	.38[c]	-.34[b]
Avoidance		
Other	-.33[b]	.38[c]
Self	-.46[c]	.46[c]
Emotional Openness	.41[c]	-.39[c]

[a] $p < .05$
[b] $p < .01$
[c] $p < .001$

Differences Between the Self and Other Responses. After determining that some of the children did indeed produce contrasting responses between references to the self and the other child, we examined how these children differed from those with noncontrasting responses. Using the three SAT summary scores for attachment, self-reliance, and avoidance, analyses were conducted in the following way. First, each child's summary score for the other child was subtracted from the score for self on each of the three SAT components. Then, each of these component-difference scores was used to divide the children into three groups: (1) those whose self-other difference score was positive (that is, the self score was greater than the other score); (2) those whose self-other difference score was zero (that is, the self score equaled the other score); and (3) those whose self-other difference score was negative (that is, the self score was less than the other score). A series of ANOVAs was conducted to determine whether those with positive, negative, or zero difference scores for the self versus the pictured child (the other) showed differences on the separation-reunion and the emotional openness scores. The emotional openness score was included as a dependent measure in this series of analyses since it reflects a different measure of the representational model than the SAT summary scores. The results of the ANOVAs are presented in Tables 3, 4, and 5.

Self-Other Differences on the Attachment Component (High-Stress Stories). As shown in Table 3, a majority of the children (Group 3; 53 percent) received higher scores when discussing the other than when

**Table 3. Comparisons of Means of Separation-Reunion
Variables and Emotional Openness by
Difference Between Self and Other Attachment Scores**

	Group 1 (N = 10)	Group 2 (N =18)	Group 3 (N = 32)	F	Posthoc Comparison[a]
Short-separation security	6.10 (1.98)	5.50 (2.68)	5.56 (2.14)	n.s.	1 = 2 = 3
Short-separation avoidance	2.10 (1.02)	2.75 (1.50)	2.94 (1.50)	n.s.	1 = 2 = 3
Emotional openness	5.75 (2.32)	7.19 (1.77)	5.55 (2.42)	3.28^b	2 > 3, 1 = 2, 1 = 3

Note: Group 1: self-other difference score was positive; Group 2: self-other difference score was zero; Group 3: self-other difference score was negative. Parenthentical values are standard deviations of means.

[a] Duncan procedure (p = .05)

[b] $p < .05$

discussing the self. This finding suggests that, in general, these children were somewhat less able to show their feelings of sadness or regret when discussing their own feelings about separation than when referring to another child's.

Table 3 also shows that self-other differences in the SAT attachment score did not significantly differentiate the children on the two separation-reunion measures. Only the emotional openness score differed significantly between any of the three groups. Those children who received the same score for self and other (Group 2) had generally higher emotional openness scores than those whose attachment score for the other child was greater than the score for self (Group 3). The difference that showed Group 2 (self = other) to be higher than Group 1 (self greater than other) almost reached significance.

Self-Other Differences on the Self-Reliance Component (Low-Stress Stories). Table 4 presents the outcome measures in relation to the self-other difference scores on the SAT self-reliance component. These data indicated that a majority of the children (52 percent) expressed greater feelings of self-reliance when discussing the self than when discussing the other child (Group 1). However, the data indicate that the group of children who did not distinguish between discussions of the self and the other child had the most secure attachments. Specifically, the post hoc comparisons showed that those children who gave the same type of answers for the self and the other child (Group 2) had the highest security ratings, followed by children whose scores for self were higher than

Table 4. Comparisons of Means of Separation-Reunion
Variables and Emotional Openness by
Difference Between Self and Other Self-Reliance Scores

	Group 1 (N = 31)	Group 2 (N =13)	Group 3 (N = 16)	F	Posthoc Comparison[a]
Short-separation security	5.82 (2.30)	7.15 (1.78)	4.03 (1.48)	8.96[b]	2 > 1 > 3
Short-separation avoidance	2.61 (1.52)	2.35 (1.18)	3.31 (1.38)	n.s.	1 = 2 = 3
Emotional openness	6.39 (2.19)	7.38 (1.66)	4.41 (2.15)	8.11[b]	2 = 1 > 3

Note: Group 1: self-other difference score was positive; Group 2: self-other difference score was zero; Group 3: self-other difference score was negative. Parenthentical values are standard deviations of means.

[a] Duncan procedure ($p = .05$)

[b] $p < .001$

their scores for the other (Group 1). Those children whose self-reliance scores for the other child were higher than their scores for self (Group 3) were those children with the lowest attachment security ratings from the separation-reunion data. The means of the avoidance rating on reunion (in the opposite direction) also showed this trend but failed to reach statistical significance. Additionally, both Group 1 and Group 2 children received higher scores on the SAT rating of emotional openness than did Group 3.

Self-Other Differences on the Avoidance Component. The comparisons of the self-other difference variable on the SAT avoidance score are presented in Table 5. Once again, those who did not differentiate between the self and the other child (Group 2) had optimal scores on security and avoidance as well as higher emotional openness ratings for the short separation. In fact, on each of these measures Group 2 surpassed Group 1 (53 percent), who received higher avoidance scores when discussing themselves.

Implications of the Self-Other Differences and Future Directions. The data presented here suggest that the SAT responses by the children with the most secure attachments were strong reflections of their internal representations as related to their attachment behavior. This was true whether the children were asked about themselves or the children in the pictures. In contrast, the children with somewhat less secure attachments tended to make themselves appear somewhat more self-sufficient than the children in the pictures, both on the low- and high-stress separation

Table 5. Comparisons of Means of Separation-Reunion Variables and Emotional Openness by Difference Between Self and Other Avoidance Scores

	Group 1 (N = 32)	Group 2 (N =14)	Group 3 (N = 14)	F	Posthoc Comparison[a]
Short-separation security	5.00 (2.14)	7.07 (2.22)	5.64 (2.04)	4.58[b]	2 > 1; 3 = 1; 3 = 2
Short-separation avoidance	3.20 (1.59)	1.71 (.51)	2.71 (1.22)	6.12[c]	1 > 2; 3 = 1; 3 = 2
Emotional openness	5.42 (2.49)	7.61 (1.42)	6.04 (1.97)	4.93[c]	2 > 1; 3 = 1; 3 = 2

Note: Group 1: self-other difference score was positive; Group 2: self-other difference score was zero; Group 3: self-other difference score was negative. Parenthetical values are standard deviations of means.

[a] Duncan procedure ($p = .05$)

[b] $p < .01$

[c] $p < .01$

stories. The children with the least secure attachments were inclined to present the children in the pictures as more self-reliant than themselves. Not only are these results the reverse of what we found for securely attached children, but they seem to conflict with what one would expect from a typical five-year-old.

Our findings regarding differences in responding for self and other child lend support to Bowlby's (1980) proposals about defensive exclusion. The more secure the child, the less likely he or she is to make a distinction between self and peer when discussing separations from parents, suggesting that children with secure attachments can process and disclose their emotions concerning attachment-related material without regard to the referent (that is, the self or other child). However, the insecure children in this sample seemed less able to consciously process attachment-relevant information about the self. These children may have been unable to access information about themselves that conflicted with their image of an independent five-year-old, or they may have "revised" the information to coincide with this image. When discussing a hypothetical child, these five-year-olds were able to distance themselves sufficiently from the affective components of the pictures to discuss the situations from an "intellectual" viewpoint. However, when confronted with the same issues regarding themselves, the cognitive and emotional components may have been too difficult to dissociate. By avoiding discussion of the parental relationship, the children could avert the arousal of anxious thoughts and feelings.

Conceptually, avoidance and defensive processes come into play when the appraisal of a current situation activates unresolved conflicts from previous experiences. These thoughts or feelings are then not employed (that is, they are repressed) in evaluating the current situation. This may explain the generally higher correlations derived from the self data. That is, the responses about self may be more strongly related to the child's reunion behavior because both sets of data are manifestations of related aspects of the child's representations of the maternal-child relationship. Some children may demonstrate a working model of a secure, confident youngster when discussing the other child (conscious processing), but the "authentic" working model of the self is more telling of their true insecurity.

Other data from this project support our interpretation. Slough (1988) found that the self variables of the SAT were more strongly related to the child's maturity rating during a frustrating waiting task, to child and mother affect ratings, and to ratings of the child's cooperation with an examiner than were the variables referred to as the other.

Slough also suggests, however, that caution should be exercised in the assessment of preschoolers' attachment security. As mentioned earlier, besides the short-separation data reported here, child and mother also were separated for about one-and-one-half hours (the long separation), again followed by a reunion. It is curious that the long-separation-reunion assessment showed very little relationship to any SAT variables, or to other attachment-relevant data (see Slough, 1988). This may be due to specific procedures, order effects of the two separations, or child fatigue, underscoring the need for careful scrutiny of the methodology employed for attachment assessment with preschoolers.

The presentations of the self and other child reported here are considered reflections of the children's working models. The significant relationship between these reports and the children's reunion behavior with their mothers implies that the ways in which these children discussed their feelings regarding separations are a valid index of how they perceive their relationships with their parents. Children who are able to express their concern over severe separations, yet also show self-confidence in handling mild separations, are likely to perceive their parents as responsive and trustworthy (for example, "I would be a little scared, because they were leaving but I know they'll come back"). Responses that are avoidant or disturbed likewise signify how the child perceives the parental relationship (for example, "I'd be crying, 'cus she's leaving me at school all day long, [do?] kick her in the leg and tell people I hate 'em").

Assessment of the preschooler's mental representations and perceptions can be a formidable task, and research has only begun to scratch the surface of the rich and complex nature of children's working models. These findings, as well as those of others (Bretherton, Ridgeway, and

Cassidy, in press; Cassidy, 1988; Main, Kaplan, and Cassidy, 1985; Mueller and Tinsley, this volume), indicate the potential value of assessing preschoolers' internal representations by alternative methods, including both observation and a clinical-style interview involving attachment-related content. In this study we focused on how children feel and what they do in response to parental behavior (that is, parents' departures). From the children's responses, we obtained one perspective of how children perceive their relationships with the parent(s) around the sensitive issues of separation, care, and protection. It would be equally interesting to have the children talk directly about how their parents would feel about separations and what their parents would do. The children might also be asked how the parents would tell them about the impending separation, in what manner they would depart (for example, say good-bye, give a kiss, sneak away), and what might happen when the parents returned. Certainly, exploration of preschoolers' internal working models from a variety of perspectives will lead to deeper understanding of how children perceive their affective relationships with their parents and how those perceptions influence their interpersonal relationships with others.

References

Ainsworth, M. D. "Epilogue." In M. Greenberg, M. Cummings, and D. Cicchetti (eds.), *Attachment Beyond the Preschool Years*. Chicago: University of Chicago Press, in press.

Bowlby, J. *Attachment and Loss*. Vol. 2: *Separation*. New York: Basic Books, 1973.

Bowlby, J. *Attachment and Loss*. Vol. 3: *Loss, Sadness, and Depression*. New York: Basic Books, 1980.

Bowlby, J. *Attachment and Loss*. Vol. 1: *Attachment*. (Rev. ed.) New York: Basic Books, 1982. (Originally published 1969.)

Bretherton, I., Ridgeway, D., and Cassidy, J. "The Role of Internal Working Models in the Attachment Relationship: A Story Completion Task for 3-Year-Olds." In M. Greenberg, M. Cummings, and D. Cicchetti (eds.), *Attachment Beyond the Preschool Years*. Chicago: University of Chicago Press, in press.

Cassidy, J. "Child-Mother Attachment and the Self in Six-Year-Olds." *Child Development*, 1988, *59*, 121–134.

Cassidy, J., and Kobak, R. R. "Avoidance and Its Relation to Other Defensive Processes." In J. Belsky and T. Nezworski (eds.), *Clinical Implications of Attachment*. Hillsdale, N.J.: Erlbaum, 1988.

Crnic, K. A., Ragozin, A. S., Greenberg, M. T., Robinson, N. M., and Basham, R. B. "Effects of Stress and Social Support on Mothers and Premature and Full-Term Infants." *Child Development*, 1983, *54*, 209–217.

Hansburg, H. G. *Adolescent Separation Anxiety: A Method for the Study of Adolescent Separation Problems*. Springfield, Ill.: C. C. Thomas, 1972.

Kaplan, N. "Internal Representations of Separation Experiences in Six-Year-Olds: Related to Actual Experiences of Separation." Unpublished master's thesis, Department of Psychology, University of California, Berkeley, 1984.

Klagsbrun, M., and Bowlby, J. "Responses to Separation for Parents: A Clinical Test for Young Children." *British Journal of Projective Psychology and Personality Study*, 1976, *21*, 7–27.

84   CHILDREN'S PERSPECTIVES ON THE FAMILY

Main, M., and Cassidy, J. "Assessment of Child-Parent Attachment at Six Years of Age." Unpublished manuscript, University of California, Berkeley, 1985.

Main, M., and Cassidy, J. "Categories of Response to Reunion with the Parent at Age 6: Predictable from Infant Attachment Classifications and Stable over a One-Month Period." *Journal of Developmental Psychology*, 1988, *24*, 415–426.

Main, M., Kaplan, N., and Cassidy, J. "Security in Infancy, Childhood, and Adulthood: A Move to the Level of Representation." In I. Bretherton and E. Waters (eds.), *Growing Points of Attachment: Theory and Research. Monographs for the Society of Research in Child Development*, 1985, *50* (1–2, serial no. 209).

Slough, N. M. "Assessment of Attachment in Five-Year-Olds: Relationships Among Separation, the Internal Representation, and Mother-Child Functioning." Unpublished doctoral dissertation, Department of Psychology, University of Washington, Seattle, 1988.

Stern, D. *The Interpersonal World of the Infant.* New York: Basic Books, 1986.

Winnicott, D. *The Maturational Processes and the Facilitating Environment.* New York: International Universities Press, 1965.

Nancy M. Slough is coordinator for program evaluation and community outreach at the Child Development and Mental Retardation Center at the University of Washington, Seattle.

Mark T. Greenberg is associate professor of psychology at the University of Washington, Seattle.

Children at thirty-seven and fifty-four months of age were able to represent aspects of the parent-child relationship, but the older children also elaborated other family relationships and roles.

Family Relationships as Represented in a Story-Completion Task at Thirty-Seven and Fifty-Four Months of Age

Inge Bretherton, Charlynn Prentiss, Doreen Ridgeway

In formulating his theory of egocentrism, Piaget (1951) drew attention to striking qualitative differences between adults' and young children's understanding of interpersonal processes. Indeed, he depicted young children's limitations to be so severe that for a while other researchers were deterred from further exploring this area. Soon, however, a growing suspicion that childhood egocentrism was less profound than Piaget had assumed led to a flurry of investigations on the development of role taking and related forms of social understanding.

Intersubjective Understanding

We now know that infants as young as nine months of age understand that they can purposefully convey their intentions to another person and know how to establish and maintain a joint focus of attention with a partner (for example, Bretherton and Bates, 1979; Bruner, 1975; Scaife and

This research was supported by the John D. and Catherine T. MacArthur Foundation Research Network on Early Childhood Transitions. We thank Susan Codega, Christina Fuhr, Bryan Ockert, Jackie Stedtman, Linda Szabo, and Linda Wilcox for helping with data collection and transcription. We are also deeply grateful to the families who participated in the study.

Bruner, 1975; Trevarthen and Hubley, 1979). By end of the second year, just into the multiword stage, many toddlers already label and converse about a limited range of mental experiences in self and other (Bretherton and Beeghly-Smith, 1982; Dunn, Bretherton, and Munn, 1987). They also comfort distressed children and adults (Zahn-Waxler, Radke-Yarrow, and King, 1979) and show rudiments of role understanding in pretend play (Bretherton, 1984; Nicolich, 1977; Miller and Garvey, 1984; Watson and Fischer, 1980; Wolf, 1982). In the course of the third year these abilities grow by leaps and bounds (Bretherton, Fritz, Zahn-Waxler, and Ridgeway, 1986; Ridgeway, Waters and Kuczaj, 1985; Shatz, Wellman, and Silber, 1983; Wolf, Rygh, and Altshuler, 1984). At this age children also begin to argue about social rules with their mothers and siblings in everyday situations (Dunn, 1988). By three years of age, children can infer a story character's emotions in hypothetical situations (Borke, 1971) and can provide plausible reasons why a story character might feel sad, happy, or angry (for example, Trabasso, Stein, and Johnson, 1981). In addition, they have some grasp of the distinction between reality and thought (Wellman, 1988). By age four, if not before, children understand the "false belief" concept (Chandler, Fritz, and Hala, 1989; Wimmer and Perner, 1983) and the appearance-reality distinction (Flavell, Flavell, and Green, 1983). Taken together, these studies suggest that whereas Piaget (1951) was correct in pinpointing the preschool years as a period during which social understanding developed, he had clearly underestimated the level of interpersonal knowledge children possess before age seven or eight.

The Development of Relationship Understanding

While there is fairly extensive empirical evidence regarding children's developing understanding of interpersonal mental processes in self and others, our knowledge about their understanding of interpersonal relationships is still meager. In order to grasp the essence of relationships, a child has to know something about stable relationship qualities, a presumably more difficult task than understanding more transitory states of mind. The few available studies on the psychological aspects of children's relationship knowledge have concentrated on friendships with peers or on authority relations with parents.

To tap into children's friendship knowledge, researchers have asked children to talk about "how you show someone that you are friends" (Youniss and Volpe, 1978), or to define "a best friend" (Berndt, 1981). Others have relied on friendship-relevant dilemmas, followed by a series of searching questions (Damon, 1977; Selman, 1976). All of these studies suggest that children up to about age seven tend to understand best friends in behavioral terms as "someone who plays with me" or "someone who gives me toys." If psychological terms are used, they are tautological, for example, a friend is "someone who is nice (or fun)." Only children over seven years of age mention more abstract concepts such as helping and trusting one another when talking about best friends (Damon, 1977).

The studies of authority relations with parents (Damon, 1977) also portray preschoolers' relationship knowledge as quite limited. When asked to answer a series of questions about a story dilemma in which parental demand for obedience (cleaning of the child's room) conflicts with the child's wishes (to go to a picnic with a friend), four-year-olds equated the importance of parental commands with that of their own wishes: the child need only obey parents when he or she wanted to, and the parents would not insist on obedience under such circumstances. Between four and five years of age, there seemed to be more respect for authority, but children still claimed that disobedience was alright provided they could get away with it. Obedience out of respect for parents, as postulated by Piaget (1932), only occurred in children over five years of age.

Pitted against the findings from social cognitive studies on interpersonal processes, preschoolers' relationship descriptions appear curiously simplistic. Ought we therefore to conclude that relationship concepts such as loyalty, trust, or closeness are absent from the mental lives of children under seven years of age? We do not think so. Rather, we believe that the systematic questioning techniques used in studies of friendship and parental role understanding may be too demanding to reveal such smatterings of psychologically based relationship understanding as do exist. Other chapters in this volume corroborate this hypothesis: when children are observed in highly supported (scaffolded) situations, they seem quite knowledgeable about family relationships. However, so far such studies have not followed children longitudinally. Hence we still lack a developmental account of how the children's representations of family relationships change with age.

Careful developmental documentation of children's stories about relationships is important for two reasons. First, the more open-ended methods supported by props, pictures, and guiding questions tend to elicit nascent, still-fragile understandings, emphasizing what the child knows rather than what he or she does not know. In contrast, the more stringent interview and questioning techniques used by Damon and Selman emphasize solid knowledge that can withstand cognitive challenges. To fully understand young children's thinking about family and other close relationships, we need information about both types of knowledge throughout the preschool and school years. Second, if children's portrayals of family life in story-telling tasks reflect something about qualitative differences in actual family experiences (as suggested by Mueller and Tingley as well as Slough and Greenberg, this volume), we must learn to interpret performances at different ages in the context of what is usual and expectable at each age. This is especially true if we are to use similar narrative techniques with atypical populations such as maltreated or other at-risk children.

In this study we therefore decided to explore developmental differences in preschoolers' narrative performances elicited during the task of attachment story completions with family dolls at thirty-seven months and fifty-four months of age. Issues presented in the attachment stories ranged from spilling juice at the dinner table, getting hurt, and fearing a monster, to separation from and reunion with parents. In addition, we considered children's responses to a more complex story at fifty-four months, a moral dilemma (adapted from Buchsbaum and Emde, 1989). In this dilemma parental authority is in conflict not with selfish pleasure (as in Damon's 1977 study) but rather with a sibling's need for help. We were interested in (1) developmental differences in how the children resolved the issues presented in the story stems and (2) developmental changes in the complexity of family interactions and relationships as represented in scaffolded family narratives.

Method

Sample. The children and parents in this study had already taken part in a longitudinal investigation of attachment, mastery motivation, and affect communication (Maslin, Bretherton, and Morgan, 1986; Bretherton, Ridgeway, and Cassidy, in press). The families were originally identified through newspaper birth announcements, contacted by letter, and, a few days later, called on the telephone. Eighty percent of parents thus contacted were recruited to the study. Of the original thirty-six families seen at eighteen and twenty-five months, twenty-nine families were able to take part in a follow-up study at thirty-seven months; twenty-five families were still available at fifty-four months (the remainder had either moved away or, in a few cases, were unable to participate for personal reasons). This study is based on the twenty-five families who participated when their children (thirteen girls and twelve boys) were at thirty-seven and fifty-four months of age.

Other data about the parent-child attachment relationship and the family were available from earlier phases of the study. Strange Situation classifications (Ainsworth, Blehar, Waters, and Wall, 1978) had been obtained at eighteen months, Attachment Q-sorts (Waters and Deane, 1985) were performed by the mother at twenty-five and thirty-seven months, and ratings of maternal sensitivity/insight were available from a Parent Attachment Interview administered to the mother at twenty-five months (Bretherton and others, 1989). A separation-reunion procedure (Cassidy, Marvin, and MacArthur Attachment Work Group, 1987) followed the story completions at thirty-seven months. In addition, the mother had filled out the Spanier Dyadic Adjustment Scale at eighteen and at twenty-five months (Spanier, 1976) and the Family Adaptability and Cohesion Evaluation Scale (FACESII) at twenty-five months (Olson, Bell, and Portner, 1983).

Procedure. The thirty-seven-month and fifty-four-month phases of this study included a laboratory visit and a home visit. The attachment story-completion task, which is the focus of this chapter, was administered during the laboratory visits at both ages (along with mother-child and tester-child play sessions, a separation-reunion procedure, and an affect communication task). The sessions took place in a carpeted playroom furnished with a table, small chairs, and a beanbag seat. Each session was videotaped in its entirety.

After a brief encounter with the tester at the beginning of the session, mother and child spent about ten minutes engaged in free play with toys. The tester then returned, joining mother and child in additional free play. When the child seemed comfortable (usually after five to ten minutes, but longer if the child was very shy), the mother was asked to sit in a corner of the room to fill out a questionnaire while the tester cleared away the toys and arranged the small table and chairs for the child and herself.

The administration of the task began with a warm-up story about a birthday party to make sure that the child understood what was required of her or him. Five attachment-related story beginnings were then narrated and acted out for the children by the tester, using small family figures and props. A mother, father, and two child figures were used for the first three stories, and a grandmother figure was added for the final two stories. During the last story, which was administered only at fifty-four months, the mother and two child figures were used. The two sibling figures—one larger than the other—were always of the same sex as the subject (for detailed procedural instructions, see the Appendix in Bretherton, Ridgeway, and Cassidy, in press).

The five attachment story beginnings introduced the following attachment-related themes:

1. *Spilled juice* (props: parents, two children, table, small dishes and cups): While the family is having a meal, the younger child reaches across the table for a cup and accidentally spills his/her juice on the floor, and the mother says, "Oh, you spilled your juice." Issue: the parents as attachment and authority figures in relation to the child.

2. *Hurt knee* (props: parents, two children, a piece of green felt to represent grass, a sponge cut to look like a rock): While the family is taking a walk in the park, the younger child tells the parents (who are standing at a distance away) that he/she can climb the high rock. While climbing, the child falls off, hurts one knee, and cries. Issue: pain as an elicitor of child attachment and parental comforting behavior.

3. *Monster in the bedroom* (props: parents, two children, bed, blanket): After one of the children is sent upstairs to go to bed, he/she cries out to the parents downstairs about a monster. Issue: fear/danger as an elicitor of child attachment and parental protective behavior.

4. *Departure* (props: parents, grandmother, two children, a piece of green felt to represent the front lawn, a box painted to represent a car): The parents announce that they are about to leave for an overnight trip, and that the grandmother will look after the two children. Issues: the children's separation anxiety and coping ability; the grandmother as substitute parent.

5. *Reunion* (props used in departure story): Grandmother looks out of the window the next morning and announces that the parents are coming back. Issue: welcoming versus avoidant or angry reunion behavior by children and parents.

In addition, we used the following, more complex story stem, portraying the conflict between obedience to a mother's command and a sibling's need for caregiving: *Moral dilemma* (administered only at fifty-four months; props: mother, two children, shelf, bathtub, toybox with miniature toys): While the children are playing, the mother announces that she has to go to the store, and that the children are not to touch anything on the bathroom shelf while she is gone. The children acknowledge their mother's request. After mother leaves, the children play with toys in the toy box. Then the younger child cuts a finger and plaintively asks the older to "get me a Band-Aid quick." The older child replies, "But Mommy said not to touch anything on the bathroom shelf," whereupon the younger reiterates, "But my finger is bleeding." (This story was adapted from a similar dilemma used with three-year-olds by Buchsbaum and Emde, 1989.)

After presenting each of these stories according to the standard protocol, the tester asked the subject to "show me and tell me what happens next." In addition, three types of prompts were used for the five attachment stories. The first type of prompt focused on the story issue and was used only if the subject failed to address it (for example, "What did they do about the juice?"). The second type of prompt was used for clarification if the subject talked about unspecified agents ("Who put on the Band-Aid?") or moved the figures without describing their action ("What is he/she doing?"). The third type of prompt was designed to elicit elaboration ("Did anything else happen?"), unless the child indicated by speech or gesture that the story was finished. The prompts were carefully worded so as not to suggest specific responses to the child.

For the moral dilemma story, adapted from Buchsbaum and Emde (1989), the issue prompts were more complex than those used for the attachment stories (the other types of prompts were similar across all of the stories). If the subject took the simple way out by asking that the mother be brought back, the tester replied that she was still at the store. If the subject had one of the children contravene the mother's injunction, the tester asked, "Why did he/she do that when Mommy said not to touch anything on the bathroom shelf?" If the subject failed to enact a helping response, he or she was reminded, "But Bob/Jane's finger is bleeding." When the tester brought the mother back, she was made to announce, "I'm home." Only when the subjects did not mention the mishap, did the tester have the mother figure ask if the children had obeyed.

Data Analysis. The videotaped story completions were transcribed onto a coding sheet with two columns: a verbatim record of the subjects' narratives and tester's prompts in column 1 and information about the physical placement of family figures in relation to each other in column 2. Column 2 also contained descriptions of the subjects' emotional responses during high points of the story stem presentations (for example, smiling, pouting, or frowning), as well as emotional components of subjects' enactments (for example, aggressive, angry, or gentle placement or movement of the family figures; sad or happy facial expression, tone of voice, or posture). Three research assistants worked on each transcript at each age of testing. The first assistant recorded only verbal utterances, the second transcribed behavior (including emotion) and checked the accuracy of the verbal record, and the third checked the behavioral record, indicating disagreements and (much more often) filling in omitted material. This procedure, rather than independent coding with reliability checks, was adopted because the behavior transcribed was so multifaceted. Collaborative coding assured a more complete (and hence meaningful) record.

Bretherton, Ridgeway, and Cassidy (in press) examined the story completions of the subjects at thirty-seven months with respect to individual differences in the quality of attachment relationships portrayed across all five stories. Positive scores were assigned when the children addressed the story issues openly and produced benign resolutions in which the parents were depicted as caring and the child as competent. Negative scores were given if the children sidestepped the story issues, could not provide resolutions, or enacted highly unusual or violent endings (such as abandonment or car crashes). Like other authors (for example, Mueller and Tingley, this volume; Oppenheim, 1989; Slough and Greenberg, this volume), we found significant correlations between the attachment story ratings and a number of other attachment and family measures: Strange Situation classifications at eighteen months, security scores derived from the Waters and Deane (1985) Attachment Q-sorts at twenty-five months, sensitivity/insight ratings of a Parent Attachment Interview at twenty-five months, a separation-reunion procedure at thirty-seven months, and family cohesion and adaptability scores based on the FACESII at twenty-five months. A similar analysis is planned for the fifty-four-month phase of the study.

A second analysis of the transcripts focused on the content and structure of each attachment story resolution at thirty-seven and fifty-four months and of the moral dilemma at fifty-four months. In this analysis we also examined the complexity of family interactions and role differentiations. Intercoder reliability for assignment of behavior to specific categories was 95 percent for the thirty-seven-month transcripts and 92 percent for the fifty-four-month transcripts. Disagreements were resolved by discussion. This chapter is based on the second analysis.

Results and Discussion

As a group, even the thirty-seven-month-old children understood the focal issues presented in the first five stories, and most were able to enact appropriate resolutions. The most striking developmental change between thirty-seven months and fifty-four months was the increasing differentiation with which family roles were portrayed and the greater complexity of family interactions that were not directly suggested by the content of the story stems. To avoid possible confusion, the term subject is used throughout this section to identify the responding child, while the terms child, mother, father, and grandmother refer to the story figures.

The Parent-Child Relationship. The five attachment stories depicted the doll family in a variety of common situations that elicit caregiving, discipline, empathic concern, and reassurance from parents and care seeking, fear of discipline, and separation anxiety from children.

In terms of the issues presented in the attachment stories, there were surprisingly few differences between story resolutions at the earlier and at the later ages of the subjects. Both the thirty-seven- and fifty-four-month-olds differentiated between the mother and the father roles. In the spilled juice story, subjects chose the mother over the father for cleaning up ($N = 9$ versus $N = 2$ at thirty-seven months; $N = 12$ versus $N = 3$ at fifty-four months) and for administering discipline by spanking, time-out, verbal reproach, or anger ($N = 5$ versus $N = 0$ at thirty-seven months; $N = 8$ versus $N = 4$ at fifty-four months). Subjects also preferred the mother for "reparative" nurturant behavior, for example, pouring more juice ($N = 3$ versus $N = 0$ at thirty-seven months; ($N = 3$ versus $N = 1$ at fifty-four months). In the hurt knee story, subjects chose the mother more frequently for caregiving behaviors, sometimes by picking up the hurt child and holding her or him, but more often by putting on a Band-Aid ($N = 7$ versus $N = 1$ at thirty-seven months; $N = 11$ versus $N = 7$ at fifty-four months).

The protector role in the monster story, by contrast, was preferentially allotted to the father, who more often than the mother disposed of the monster through various means (shooting, killing, or throwing it, chasing it out of the room, chopping it up, ripping it to shreds, and so forth). This preference for the father as protector became especially pronounced at fifty-four months ($N = 5$ versus $N = 9$ at thirty-seven months; $N = 2$ versus $N = 13$ at fifty-four months).

Aggregated over the first three attachment stories, subjects' use of the father in at least one story rose significantly with age ($N = 10$ at thirty-seven months versus $N = 18$ at fifty-four months; sign test, $p < .03$). A corresponding increase occurred in the number of subjects who used both parents cooperatively, for example, the father held the child while the mother put on the Band-Aid, or both killed the monster together ($N = 3$ versus $N = 9$; sign test, $p < .04$). There was no age difference in the number of subjects who used the mother in these roles. Perhaps not surprisingly, the fifty-four-month-olds had the parents enact more verbal than nonverbal behavioral interventions (for example, parental admonishments about the spilled juice and hurt knee and denials of the monster's existence; $N = 4$ versus $N = 11$; sign test, $p < .02$). One precocious thirty-seven-month-old specifically had the mother state that she would *not* punish the child for falling off the rock (hence deliberately differentiating her response in the hurt knee story from that in the spilled juice story where she had mildly spanked the child) but this type of statement was more typical of fifty-four-month-olds.

Whereas resolutions for the first three stories focused primarily on the parents' behaviors and feelings of anger or concern, the converse was true of the two separation stories, where the children's behaviors and feelings came to the fore. However, as had been the case for the first three stories, thirty-seven-month-olds and fifty-four-month-olds produced remarkably similar types of resolutions in response to the departure and the reunion story stems. A substantial number of subjects ($N = 14$ at thirty-seven months versus $N = 13$ at fifty-four months) portrayed the children's reluctance at letting the parents leave, primarily by trying to have them (and the grandmother) join the departing parents in the car. This solution was not permitted by the tester, who countered, "But I thought only the mommy and daddy are going." In addition, 2 fifty-four-month-olds had the younger child cry as the parents left. Subjects' own anxieties shone through as they protested the tester's attempts to remove the car from the scene, for example, "Nope, they're not going."

While the parents were away, a small number of subjects expressed separation anxiety by having the children search for, cry for, or think about the absent parents ($N = 7$ at thirty-seven months versus $N = 5$ at fifty-four months), for example, "The girls run after the car because they want their Mom and Dad," "They think their Mom and Dad are gone," and "They walk on the street to find their Mom and Dad," and through anticipating the parents' return verbally and/or retrieving the parental car (from under the table) before the tester had time to begin the reunion story ($N = 6$ at thirty-seven months versus $N = 5$ at fifty-four months).

Aggregating the data over the departure and separation stories, 18 thirty-seven-month-olds and 16 fifty-four-month-olds exhibited one or more behaviors indicative of separation anxiety or longing for the parents.

When the tester brought the parents' car back, most subjects reunited the family. At thirty-seven months this consisted mostly of driving the car back home, taking the parens out, and placing them near the children. Hugging and other forms of affection occurred, but less often than we had expected ($N = 2$ at thirty-seven months versus $N = 3$ at fifty-four months). However, fifty-four-month-olds enacted significantly more verbal greetings or conversations by the children, ranging from a simple "Hi" to "We missed you" and "Did you have a good time?" ($N = 5$ versus $N = 15$; sign test, $p < .01$).

Other developmental differences were evidenced by themes in story content that were not directly suggested by the story stems, although they were inspired by the presence of the five family figures: the husband-wife relationship, the sibling relationship, and the role of the grandmother.

The Husband-Wife Relationship. At fifty-four months, 9 subjects portrayed parental activities apart from the children (for example, conversing with each other, planning an outing to a restaurant, watching television, going for a walk, and going to sleep), whereas only 3 subjects did so at thirty-seven months (sign test, $p < .004$). This kind of parental activity occurred particularly frequently during the monster stories and occasionally during the hurt knee and departure stories.

Child Roles and the Sibling Relationship. An equivalent number of thirty-seven- and fifty-four-month-olds had the siblings engage in joint behavior such as playing, fighting, sleeping, searching for the parents, or welcoming them home ($N = 22$ versus $N = 24$ at, respectively). Significant age differences did emerge, however, in the differentiation of the older and younger sibling roles. We examined two categories of behavior: (1) having the older sibling act more competent or mature (or the younger act more babyish or less competent) and (2) portraying the older sibling in a quasi-parental role. With respect to the first category, the older child managed to drink her or his juice without spilling it during the spilled juice story (for example, "Because she was more careful"). In the hurt knee story, the older child climbed the rock without falling off (for example, "Because she's bigger"). In the departure story, the younger child (never the older) cried or asked not to be left behind as the parents departed. Aggregated over stories, these differences were highly significant ($N = 5$ at thirty-seven months versus $N = 17$ at fifty-four months; sign test, $p < .002$).

As regards quasi-parental roles of the older sibling, the only behaviors that could possibly be categorized in this fashion at thirty-seven months consisted of placing the younger child next to the older child after the fall from the rock or having the older sibling kiss the younger, hurt sibling. The fifty-four-month-olds, by contrast, portrayed various quasi-parental behaviors by the older child toward the younger child. For example, the older held or verbally reassured the younger in the hurt knee, monster, and departure stories, and in the monster story the younger child wanted the older to sleep with him/her after the monster was gone. One fifty-four-month-old subject enacted teaching behavior on the part of the older sibling (showing the younger child how to climb the rock successfully), and another portrayed disciplinary actions (the older sibling admonishing the younger child for spilling juice). The age difference for quasi-parental behavior was significant ($N = 3$ versus $N = 11$; sign test, $p < .03$). Aggregating over categories, the mean frequency of both categories of behavior (treating the older sibling as more mature and/or as quasi-parental) also increased substantially in the stories from thirty-seven to fifty-four months ($M = .20$ versus $M = 1.5$; Wilcoxon matched-pairs signed-ranks test, $p < .001$).

The Role of the Grandmother. There was a significant age change in portrayals of the grandmother role during the departure story. The thirty-seven-month-olds who explicitly used or talked about the grandmother tended to depict her as a companion (for example, she stayed with the children, she slept with the children, and, in one case, she called for the parents with the children). This type of behavior was less frequent at fifty-four months ($N = 10$ versus $N = 3$; sign test, $p < .06$). Instead, more fifty-four-month-olds used the grandmother in an explicitly parental role (for example, she cooked for the children, sent them out to play, comforted them when one of them got hurt, and disciplined the older sibling for interfering in the activities of the younger; $N = 2$ versus $N = 10$; sign test, $p < .003$). During the reunion story, a small number of subjects at both ages ($N = 3$ at thirty-seven months versus $N = 7$ at fifty-four months) wanted to remove the grandmother from the scene or had the family take her home, indications of their understanding that she was not part of the nuclear family. Although the age difference was not significant, the behavior was much more explicitly described as "taking grandma home" or "giving her back to her family" at the later age. One subject claimed the grandmother could not hold the "baby" younger child because she (the grandmother) was too old.

The Family. Many subjects at both ages ended their stories with family activities. For example, after cleaning up the spilled juice, the family ate together or washed the dishes; after putting a Band-Aid on the hurt knee, the family went for a walk together; after the monster was gone, all family members went to sleep; and after the reunion (when this type of behavior was part of the story), the family either went on an outing such as visiting a pizza establishment, going to church, driving home to eat supper, or taking grandmother home ("They're going to give the grandma back to her family") or engaged in an activity at home such as eating, baking, having a party, having friends over, and going to sleep. There was a significant increase from thirty-seven to fifty-four months in the frequency of endings involving family "togetherness" ($M = 0.60$ at thirty-seven months versus $M = 1.64$ at fifty-four months; Wilcoxon matched-pairs signed-ranks test, $p < .0001$). These benign endings seemed designed to restore family harmony or unity after the various mishaps and disturbances. Unhappy endings involving the whole family (for example, abandonment, car crash, death) were extremely rare in this sample ($N = 1$ at thirty-seven months versus $N = 3$ at fifty-four months).

A second form of behavior related to family togetherness consisted of replaying the hurt knee story, with or without the mishap. During this story, 4 thirty-seven-month-olds and 6 fifty-four-month-olds made both children and one or both parents jump off the rock (there were also some reenactments involving the children only). In about half of the reenactments all family members fell, in the other half the family successfully climbed the rock. The tendency to reenact the disturbance or mishap was much rarer during the monster and reunion stories (no monster replays at thirty-seven months, and three at fifty-four months; one full separation story replay at both ages), perhaps because these stories were perceived as more threatening than the others.

Story Complexity. Although similar types of story resolutions were produced by the younger and older subjects (the parents cleaned up the juice and/or punished the child, the parents put a Band-Aid on the hurt child, the parents disposed of the monster, and so forth), there were very obvious differences between the two age groups in overall narrative quality. The use of character speech (number of family members for whom the subject talked) increased significantly from thirty-seven to fifty-four months ($M = 1.16$ versus $M = 2.56$; Wilcoxon matched-pairs signed-ranks test, $p < .0001$). The frequency of back-and-forth conversations among the protagonists (for example, the children boasting to each other about how tough they are while wrestling on the lawn; the parents discussing to which restaurant they should go on the day after getting rid of the monster) also rose significantly ($M = 0.28$ versus $M = 1.08$, Wilcoxon matched-pairs signed-ranks test, $p < .0001$). Moreover, far fewer subjects intervened in the events of the stories or failed to clarify the identity of the agents at fifty-four months than did so at thirty-seven months ($N = 12$ at thirty-seven months versus $N = 2$ at fifty-four months; sign test, $p < .006$).

Subjects' representations of the flow of time also became more sophisticated. Significantly more fifty-four-month-olds than thirty-seven-month-olds referred to the next day or to waking or getting up again ($N = 3$ at thirty-seven months versus $N = 9$ at fifty-four months; sign test, $p < .02$). However, despite impressive gains in language development, the frequency with which subjects mentioned feelings, feeling expressions, or moral judgments of the protagonists remained constant $M = 1.9$ versus

M = 2.2). These particular data may seem counterintuitive at first glance, but the results are probably due to the fact that, at the older age, emotions were expressed directly through paralinguistic features of character talk (for example, instead of saying the mother was angry, subjects had her talk in an angry voice).

Finally, quantitative data, though interesting, do not adequately reflect the quality of many of the fifty-four-month-olds' narratives. Here, examples better illustrate narrative performance. For instance, in the hurt knee story, one fifty-four-month-old boy had the hurt child climb the rock again and almost fall off. He then commented, "This is a lesson story, what teaches you a lesson." He proceeded to narrate the boy's struggle to keep hanging onto the rock and his careful descent to "where it's safer." Another subject had the children keep looking for the monster during the departure story. When the parents returned, they and the children drove off together to continue the search, while the grandmother guarded the house. The family followed the footsteps of the monster, found its body, loaded it into the car, and drove home. Also in response to the departure story, one fifty-four-month-old had the grandmother send the younger child to bed while the older stayed up with her. However, the younger child stayed awake until the grandmother and older sibling fell asleep and then "sneaked out to find Mom and Dad."

The Moral Dilemma Story. This story was more complex than the attachment stories because it explicitly probed for subjects' abilities to cope with the conflicting demands of two family-internal relationships (child to mother and child to sibling). Unfortunately, we did not administer this story to the thirty-seven-month-olds. We include it here to demonstrate that scaffolding provided by a complex story stem can help more clearly illuminate the full range of subjects' abilities to represent family relationships. Remember that four-year-olds, in response to a somewhat different verbal dilemma presented by Damon (1977), conveyed the belief that there is no need to obey parents when one does not want to.

We believe that all of our subjects understood that the moral dilemma story presented them (and the story child) with a quandary. The initial response of nine subjects to "What happens next" was to ask for the mother to come back (she could then put the Band-Aid on the younger child and save the older child from having to break the parental prohibition). The tester was instructed not to allow this easy way out (by saying, "But Mommy is still at the store").

Having to handle the situation in the absence of the mother, two subjects produced what we call a mature, integrated solution. The older sibling obtained the Band-Aid from the forbidden shelf, but the returning mother expressly stated that she was not going to punish the disobedient child ("That was alright, if she hurted herself" and "I'm still not going to spank you"). In short, these two subjects seemed to have some under-

standing that rules are not inviolable provided there is good justification
for breaking them. A third subject had the older child phone the mother
at the store whereby he obtained permission to "take only the Band-Aid,
nothing else." Here the mother was asked to grant an exception to the
rule before going ahead.

Somewhat less mature, but still integrating both the mother's request
and the siblings' need, were the solutions of three subjects who had the
older child find a Band-Aid from a different location in the house (for
example, the child's room or the kitchen). One of these subjects initially
tried to eliminate the whole dilemma. The younger child was not really
hurt. A toy had fallen on his arm without really hurting him, therefore
only a pretend Band-Aid was required. When this solution was rejected
by the tester, the subject had the older child find a Band-Aid in the
bedroom. Another three subjects had the younger child invent an alternative strategy for dealing with the bleeding finger (for example, holding
the cut finger under a running faucet).

Of the remaining sixteen subjects, one avoided the issue altogether.
The other fifteen produced two juxtaposed solutions instead of a single
integrated one. Although less advanced, these juxtaposed solutions indicated that the mother's injunction *and* the hurt sibling's need had been
understood. Fourteen subjects had the older child get the Band-Aid for
the younger, but with subsequent punishment (time-out, spanking, or
verbal reprimand) when mother returned home. One of these subjects
had the older sibling correctly predict that she was going to get in trouble
as she put the forbidden Band-Aid on the younger. Another enacted
"immanent justice" (Piaget, 1932) by making the shelf fall down, as if in
punishment, as the child took the Band-Aid. Another subject seemed
motivated by a sense of unfair punishment. She had the younger sibling
defend the older: "I cut my finger and Susan got a Band-Aid, and she
didn't mean it for putting it on me. O.k. can she get out of her room?"

Most subjects ($N = 22$) had the returning mother discover the Band-
Aid and wound, by either being told ($N = 12$), having it shown to her
($N = 2$), having her ask about it ($N = 3$), or having her notice it on her
own ($N = 5$), a further index of dilemma awareness. Only two subjects
treated the mother as omniscient. These two enacted punishment of the
older child without first having the mother notice or ask about the Band-
Aid. One subject had the older sibling tell a lie, detected by the mother
when she noticed the Band-Aid. In terms of sibling relations, it is especially interesting that the child who informed the mother about the mishap and Band-Aid was usually the younger child, not the perpetrator of
disobedience. The punished child was the one who had put on the Band-
Aid (always the older child). Finally, in those cases ($N = 7$) where the
younger child had not been helped or had to make do with an unsatis-
factory alternative (such as holding the finger under a running faucet),

the mother put on the Band-Aid later, proof again that the subjects had recognized the two conflicting claims in the story stem.

The reasons given for taking the Band-Aid from the forbidden shelf were "because her finger was bleeding" ($N = 2$) or because the younger sibling wanted it ($N = 2$), whereas the reason for not helping or using alternative helping strategies was "because Mom said no touching on the bathroom shelf" ($N = 5$), though three subjects come up with excuses ("the children didn't listen"; "they didn't promise"; "they didn't know"). Fear of punishment was mentioned as the reason only once.

As in the other stories, over half of the subjects ($N = 13$) restored family harmony by ending the story with a joint activity (for example, taking a bath).

Concluding Remarks

The story tasks described here were presented to children at thirty-seven and fifty-four months of age by a supportive adult who assisted them (1) by enacting family scenarios that they were asked to complete, (2) by focusing their attention on the major story issues, and (3) by providing additional, nonleading prompts ("Did anything else happen?"). In this scaffolded context (Vygotsky, 1978), children as young as three years of age were able to demonstrate an understanding of family relationships.

At the earlier age of testing, narrations tended to be directly related to the content of the story stems, that is, they centered on the parent-child relationship, especially the mother-child relationship. Parents were portrayed as nurturant, limit setting, and empathic by subjects at both ages, though in a few cases they were depicted as violently punitive or neglectful.

By fifty-four months, the protector role of the father had become more differentiated, and the father played a greater role overall. In addition, parents more often acted together as a couple. Furthermore, the presence of an older and a younger child figure and of a grandmother inspired narrative elaborations that were not suggested by the story stems. The fifty-four-month-olds assigned differentiated roles to the older and the younger siblings (older siblings were more competent at jumping off rocks, younger siblings cried at separation from parents, older siblings cared for and protected younger siblings). These older subjects also more explicitly portrayed the caregiving role of the grandmother during the separation story and, with respect to the parents, more often mentioned parental activities that were not child-related, as if they recognized that the mother and father had a relationship of their own. A few subjects also recognized that the grandmother was not part of the nuclear family.

With respect to the subjects' understanding of the family as a system, story endings in which family togetherness was portrayed became more frequent with age, as if the subjects were concerned not only with dyadic relationships but also with restoration of overall family unity or harmony. Finally, as already noted, older subjects more often portrayed the parents vis-à-vis the children as a cooperating couple rather than as individual parents.

In terms of the capacity to portray family members in dual roles, the contrast between the attachment stories and the moral dilemma story is especially telling. Across the five attachment stories, a sizable number of fifty-four-month-olds portrayed the same family member in two different roles, demonstrating a budding capacity for role intersection, that is, an understanding that people can occupy more than one family role, such as husband and wife versus father and mother (see Watson and Fischer, 1980). However, in the moral dilemma story, where such a dual relationship was explicitly suggested by the story stem, *all* of the fifty-four-month-olds appeared to understand the conflicting claims of two relationships within the same story (the obedience-demanding mother and the needy sibling), even if all were not able to integrate both claims into one solution. In other words, when a story stem is specifically designed to draw attention to the competing claims of two relationships, older subjects better understand the conflict than when they have to create such a plot from scratch.

In terms of children's story-telling abilities, our study corroborates recent findings about preschoolers' script knowledge (Nelson and Gruendel, 1981; Nelson, 1986). Our three-year-olds were able to present reasonably coherent accounts of familiar events (accidents, pain, fear, and separations-reunions), but the older children provided more details of these events, especially with respect to family roles not directly suggested by the story stems.

Despite this clear developmental progress, the question with which we started (in what sense do preschoolers understand family relationships?) is hard to answer unequivocally. True, parental concern, care, reassurance, and anger as well as the child's longing for the absent parents were implied in the story completions of the younger children. But in fifty-four-month-olds' productions we also observed the older sibling's concern for and superiority over the younger sibling and the caregiving role of the grandmother. Moreover, these relationships were frequently depicted via verbal behavior, for example, longing for the parents was expressed through statements such as "they looked for their Mommy and Daddy." Emotions and intentions were not always explicitly mentioned, although they were strongly suggested by the behaviors portrayed as well as in the manner in which they were acted out (for example, tone of voice and quality of movement). Therefore, whether or not one is willing to grant that an understanding of family relationships is present at the psychological level depends on the stringency of the criteria applied.

It is unlikely, for example, that the three fifty-four-month-old subjects who seemed to understand that parental injunctions can sometimes be violated (as well as the other subject at this age who seemed concerned about fairness) could have answered stringent questions about prioritizing moral claims. It is possible that those who portrayed sibling as well as parental roles would have failed Watson and Fischer's (1980) strict test of role intersection in which the dual roles were those of father-doctor and child-patient, roles not familiar to most children. Nevertheless, we suggest that the increasing differentiation of roles and the complexity of family interaction depicted in children's story completions at both ages reflect a genuinely growing, though probably still fragile, ability to think about the family both in terms of differentiated dyadic relationships and as a whole.

One remaining question concerns the meaning of *what* is represented in the story completions in this and similar studies. Like other investigators represented in this volume (Miller and Tingley; Slough and Greenberg), we had not originally devised our story technique as a social-cognitive test. Rather, our aim was to elicit narratives reflecting the quality of the children's actual family experiences (Bretherton, Ridgeway, and Cassidy, in press). Following Bowlby's (1973, 1980) theorizing about the development of "internal working models" of self and other in relationships, and based on findings from studies of event representation (Nelson, 1986; Mandler, 1979), we had hypothesized that young children's notions of family roles derive in major part from transactions within their own families (see Bretherton, in press, a and b). Hence, we assumed that in response to story stems that depicted family situations familiar to most children, that is, situations experienced in their own families, our subjects would draw on their "internal working models" of family interactions. In other words, we assumed that their story completions (directly or by sidestepping the issues) would reveal something about their representations of actual family experience, rather than merely provide information about their level of family role understanding.

A task for future research is to differentiate more clearly between these two domains of study. Narrative procedures supported by props (dolls or pictures) seem to hold great promise for gaining more insight into preschoolers' development of family role understanding *and* their perceptions of their own families. By carefully tailoring our story stems and methods of inquiry to the specific objectives at hand, by painstakingly documenting subjects' story responses at various ages, and by contrasting responses to "easy" and "difficult" stories, we will be able to differentiate better between these aspects of children's narratives that flow from individual experience in each particular family and those aspects that index social-cognitive status. For example, when the primary goal is to pinpoint children's cognitive level of family role understanding, specific, even leading questions are in order. In contrast, when individual experience is at issue, very open-minded prompting is preferable, though one might use props to suggest a variety of possible responses. In this more "projective" context, choice is of the essence and avoidance of the story issue is not a nuisance but instead provides useful information. In our study, where the attachment stories did not specifically "pull" for sibling-related material, the differentiation of older and younger sibling roles may have been played out mostly by those children for whom it was a personal concern (for example, one fifty-four-month-old consistently either eliminated or derogated the younger sibling across the stories). Thus, the attachment stories are likely to *underestimate* what subjects could produce when stories are deliberately designed to elicit sibling representations. Similarly, the fact that the issues of parental fairness and rule violability were even brought up by some of the fifty-four-month-olds in the moral dilemma suggests that when story stems are designed to elicit this kind of information, we may discover such awareness is present in a greater number of young children than previously thought. In sum, we strongly believe that clinical inferences about story completions can and must be refined in the context of advances of social-cognitive development. Conversely, findings from more clinically oriented analyses may help to generate better tests of social understanding, especially in the emotionally charged area of family relationships.

References

Ainsworth, M. D., Blehar, M. C., Waters, E., and Wall, S. *Patterns of Attachment: A Psychological Study of the Strange Situation.* Hillsdale, N.J.: Erlbaum, 1978.

Berndt, T. J. "Relationships Between Social Cognition, Nonsocial Cognition, and Social Behavior: The Case of Friendship." In J. H. Flavell and L. D. Ross (eds.), *Social Cognitive Development.* New York: Cambridge University Press, 1981.

Borke, H. "Interpersonal Perception of Young Children: Egocentrism or Empathy?" *Developmental Psychology,* 1971, *5,* 263–269.

Bowlby, J. *Attachment and Loss.* Vol. 2: *Separation.* New York: Basic Books, 1973.

Bowlby, J. *Attachment and Loss.* Vol. 3: *Loss, Sadness, and Depression.* New York: Basic Books, 1980.

Bretherton, I. "Representing the Social World in Symbolic Play: Reality and Fantasy." In I. Bretherton (ed.), *Symbolic Play: The Development of Social Understanding.* New York: Academic Press, 1984.

Bretherton, I. "Open Communication and Internal Working Models: Their Role in Attachment Relationships." In R. A. Thompson (ed.), *Socioemotional Development.* (Nebraska Symposium on Motivation, 1987.) Lincoln: University of Nebraska Press, in press, a.

Bretherton, I. "Pouring New Wine into Old Bottles: The Social Self as Internal Working Model." In M. Gunnar and L. A. Sroufe (eds.), *Self Processes.* (Minnesota Symposia on Child Psychology, 1988.) Hillsdale, N.J.: Erlbaum, in press, b.

Bretherton, I., and Bates, E. "The Emergence of Intentional Communication." In I. C. Uzgiris (ed.), *Social Interaction and Communication During Infancy.*

FAMILY RELATIONSHIPS   103

New Directions for Child Development, no. 4. San Francisco: Jossey-Bass, 1979.

Bretherton, I., and Beeghly-Smith, M. "Talking About Internal States: The Acquisition of an Explicit Theory of Mind." *Developmental Psychology*, 1982, *18*, 906–921.

Bretherton, I., Biringen, Z., Ridgeway, D., Maslin, M., and Sherman, M. "Attachment: The Parental Perspective." *Infant Mental Health Journal*, 1989, *10*, 203–221.

Bretherton, I., Fritz, J., Zahn-Waxler, C., and Ridgeway, D. "Learning to Talk About Emotions: A Functionalist Perspective." *Child Development*, 1986, *57*, 529–548.

Bretherton, I., Ridgeway, D., and Cassidy, J. "The Role of Internal Working Models in the Attachment Relationship: A Story Completion Task for 3-Year-Olds." In M. Greenberg, M. Cummings, and D. Cicchetti (eds.), *Attachment Beyond the Preschool Years*. Chicago: University of Chicago Press, in press.

Bruner, J. "The Ontogenesis of Speech Acts." *Journal of Child Language*, 1975, *2*, 1–19.

Buchsbaum, H. K., and Emde, R. N. "Play Narratives in 36-Month-Old Children: The Portrayal of Early Moral Development and Family Relationships." Unpublished manuscript, University of Colorado Health Sciences Center, 1989.

Cassidy, J., Marvin, R. S., and MacArthur Attachment Work Group. "Attachment Organization in Three- and Four-Year-Olds: Coding Guidelines." Unpublished manuscript, Department of Psychology, University of Virginia, 1987.

Chandler, M. J., Fritz, A. S., and Hala, S. M. "Small-Scale Deceit: Deception as a Marker of 2-, 3-, and 4-Year-Olds' Early Theories of Mind." *Child Development*, 1989, *60*, 1263–1277.

Damon, W. *The Social World of the Child*. San Francisco: Jossey-Bass, 1977.

Dunn, J. *The Beginnings of Social Understanding*. Cambridge, Mass.: Harvard University Press, 1988.

Dunn, J., Bretherton, I., and Munn, P. "Conversations About Feeling States Between Mothers and Their Young Children." *Developmental Psychology*, 1987, *23*, 132–139.

Flavell, J. H., Flavell, E. R., and Green, F. L. "Development of the Appearance-Reality Distinction." *Cognitive Psychology*, 1983, *15*, 95–120.

Mandler, J. H. "Categorical and Schematic Organization in Memory." In C. R. Puff (ed.), *Memory Organization and Structure*. New York: Academic Press, 1979.

Maslin, C., Bretherton, I., and Morgan, G. A. "Influence of Attachment Security and Maternal Scaffolding on Mastery Motivation." Paper presented at the International Conference on Infant Studies, Los Angeles, April 1986.

Miller, P., and Garvey, C. "Mother-Baby Role-Play: Its Origin in Social Support." In I. Bretherton (ed.), *Symbolic Play: The Development of Social Understanding*. New York: Academic Press, 1984.

Nelson, K. *Event Knowledge: Structure and Function in Development*. Hillsdale, N.J.: Erlbaum, 1986.

Nelson, K., and Gruendel, J. "Generalized Event Representations: Basic Building Blocks of Cognitive Development." In M. E. Lamb and A. Brown (eds.), *Advances in Developmental Psychology*. Vol. 1. Hillsdale, N.J.: Erlbaum, 1981.

Nicolich, L. "Beyond Sensorimotor Intelligence: Assessment of Symbolic Maturity Through Analysis of Pretend Play." *Merrill-Palmer Quarterly*, 1977, *23*, 88–99.

Olson, D. H., Bell, R., and Portner, J. "FACES II (Family Adaptability and Cohesion Evaluation Scale)." Unpublished manuscript, Department of Family Social Science, University of Minnesota, Saint Paul, 1983.

Oppenheim, D. "Assessing the Validity of a Doll Play Interview for Measuring Attachment in Preschoolers." Unpublished doctoral dissertation, University of Utah, 1989.

Piaget, J. *The Moral Judgment of the Child.* New York: Free Press, 1932.

Piaget, J. *Play, Dreams, and Imitation.* New York: Norton, 1951.

Ridgeway, D., Waters, E., and Kuczaj, S. A. "The Acquisition of Emotion Descriptive Language: Receptive and Productive Vocabulary Norms for 18 Months to 6 Years." *Developmental Psychology*, 1985, *21*, 901–908.

Scaife, M., and Bruner, J. "The Capacity for Joint Visual Attention in the Infant." *Nature*, 1975, *253*, 265–266.

Selman, R. "The Development of Interpersonal Reasoning." In A. Pick (ed.), *Minnesota Symposia on Child Psychology.* Vol. 10. Minneapolis: University of Minnesota Press, 1976.

Shatz, M., Wellman, H. M., and Silber, S. "The Acquisition of Mental Verbs: A Systematic Investigation of the First Reference to Mental State." *Cognition*, 1983, *14*, 301–321.

Spanier, G. B. "Measuring Dyadic Adjustment: New Scales for Assessing the Quality of Marriage and Similar Dyads." *Journal of Marriage and the Family*, 1976, *38*, 15–28.

Trabasso, T., Stein, N. L., and Johnson, L. R. "Children's Knowledge of Events: A Causal Analysis of Knowledge Structure." In *The Psychology of Learning and Motivation.* Vol. 15. New York: Academic Press, 1981.

Trevarthen, C., and Hubley, P. "Secondary Intersubjectivity: Confidence, Confiding, and Acts of Meaning in the First Year." In A. Lock (ed.), *Action, Gesture, and Symbol.* New York: Academic Press, 1979.

Vygotsky, L. S. *Mind in Society: The Development of Higher Psychological Processes.* Cambridge, Mass.: Harvard University Press, 1978.

Waters, E., and Deane, K. E. "Defining and Assessing Individual Differences in Attachment Relationships: Q-Methodology and the Organization of Behavior in Infancy and Early Childhood." In I. Bretherton and E. Waters (eds.), *Growing Points of Attachment: Theory and Research. Monographs of the Society for Research in Child Development.* 1985 *50* (1–2, serial no. 209).

Watson, M. W., and Fischer, K. W. "Development of Social Roles in Elicited and Spontaneous Behavior." *Developmental Psychology*, 1980, *16*, 483–494.

Wellman, H. M. "First Steps in the Child's Theorizing About the Mind." In J. Astington, P. Harris, and D. Olson (eds.), *Developing Theories of Mind.* New York: Cambridge University Press, 1988.

Wimmer, H., and Perner, J. "Beliefs About Beliefs: Representations and Constraining Function of Wrong Beliefs in Young Children's Understanding of Deception." *Cognition*, 1983, *13*, 103–128.

Wolf, D. "Understanding Others: A Longitudinal Case Study of the Concept of Independent Agency." In G. Forman (ed.), *Action and Thought: From Sensorimotor Schemes to Symbol Use.* New York: Academic Press, 1982.

Wolf, D. P., Rygh, J., and Altshuler, J. "Agency and Experience: Actions and States in Play Narratives." In I. Bretherton (ed.), *Symbolic Play: The Development of Social Understanding.* New York: Academic Press, 1984.

Youniss, J., and Volpe, J. "A Relationship Analysis of Children's Friendship." In W. Damon (ed.), *Social Cognition.* New Directions for Child Development, no. 1. San Francisco: Jossey-Bass, 1978.

Zahn-Waxler, C., Radke-Yarrow, M., and King, R. "Childrearing and Children's Prosocial Initiations Towards Victims of Distress." *Child Development*, 1979, *50*, 319–330.

Inge Bretherton is professor of child and family studies at the University of Wisconsin–Madison.

Charlynn Prentiss is a student in early childhood special education at the University of Wisconsin–Madison.

Doreen Ridgeway is presently affiliated with the State University of New York at Stony Brook.

INDEX

Age relativity, and Oedipal behavior, 32, 33; assessment of, 36
Ainsworth, M. D., 57, 64, 68, 83, 88, 102
Altshuler, J., 86, 104
Amgott-Kwan, T., 32, 35, 44
Astington, J. W., 1, 4
Attachment, 3; assessment of, 67–70, 88–101; development of, 67–68; and parent-child separation, 76–83. *See also* Family relationships, Mother-child interactions
Attachment figure, and core representations, 52, 68. *See also* Attachment
Avoidant behavior, 90. *See also* Defensive exclusion

Barrett, K. C., 65
Basham, R. B., 83
Bates, E., 85, 102
Beavin, J., 50, 65
Beeghly-Smith, M., 86, 103
Behavioral qualities, 34; subjective descriptions of, 10–14
Bell, R., 89, 103
Belsky, J., 1, 4
Berndt, T. J., 15, 22, 26, 86, 102
Blehar, M. C., 57, 64, 88, 102
Borke, H., 86, 102
Bowlby, J., 1, 4, 67, 68, 69, 71–72, 81, 83, 101
Braiker, H. B., 15, 26
Brenner, J., 50, 65
Bretherton, I., 14, 22, 33, 26, 44, 51, 52, 54, 65, 68, 82, 83, 85, 86, 88, 89, 91, 101, 102, 103
Bruner, J., 85–86, 103, 104
Buchsbaum, H. K., 88, 90, 103
Buhrmester, D., 15, 22, 26

Camaioni, L., 49, 65
Campos, J. J., 50, 65
Case method, in assessing core representations, 54–55
Cassidy, J., 35, 44, 68, 69, 71, 75, 77, 82, 83, 84, 88, 89, 91, 101, 103
Cauce, A. M., 16, 22, 26

Chandler, M. J., 86, 103
Character formation, 52. *See also* Family relationships
Child abuse: and Oedipal conflict resolution, 43; and role playing, 49
Cicchetti, D. V., 56, 65
Cochran, D., 52, 65
Cohen, S., 14, 16, 26
Complementary role relations, 31. *See also* Family roles
Conflict, and social support, 14–15, 19–22; 60
Conway, A., 31, 44
Core representations. *See* Doll play narratives, Self-image, Social concept
Crisis, family, 1. *See also* Family relationships
Crnic, K. A., 70, 83

Damon, W., 86, 87, 88, 97, 103
Dean, K. E., 88, 91, 104
Defensive exclusion, 68–79, 80–82
Devaluing, self. *See* Self-image
Developmental patterns: in how children perceive families, 6; of core representations, 18–23
Developmental research: and core representations, 51–52; difficulties of, 8
Dialogue stems. *See* Dialogue techniques, Doll play narratives, Story stems
Dialogue techniques, 1–2, 5. *See also* Dialogues About Families
Dialogues About Families, 1–2; basic assumptions of, 7, 25; descriptions of, 9–18; psychometric properties of, 13–18; rationale for, 6–9, 25; results of, 18–24; value of, 25–26
DiLalla, L. F., 33, 44
Doll-play narratives, 2; in assessing attachment, 89–101; in assessing core representations, 47, 52–64; in assessing Oedipal behavior, 34–36, 39–40; bases of, 48–52; socioemotional factors in, 56; value of, 53
Dunn, J., 1, 4, 86, 103

Liben, L. S., 32, 44
Loevinger, J., 19, 27
Longitudinal studies, value of, 3; example of, 85–102

MacArthur Attachment Work Group, 88, 103
MacArthur Network on the Transition from Infancy to Early Childhood, 54
Main, M., 68, 69, 71, 75, 82, 84
Malinowski, B., 29, 44
Mandler, J. H., 101
Marcia, J. E., 19, 27
Marcus, D. E., 32, 44
Markman, H. J., 1, 4
Marvin, R. S., 88, 103
Maslin, M., 88, 103
Miller, P., 86, 101, 103
Moral dilemma, children's reactions to, 90, 97–99
Morgan, G. A., 88, 103
Mother-child interaction, assessment of, 99; and core representations, 54–59, 62–64. See also Family relationships
Mother-Infant Project, 70
Mounts, N., 52, 65
Mueller, E., 49, 50, 65, 82, 87, 91
Munn, P., 86, 103

Nelson, K., 100, 101, 103
Nicolich, L., 86, 103

Oedipal behavior, 1, 2; assessment of, 33–36; development of, 32–33, 36–38, 41; precursors to, 31–32; prevalence of, 31, 41–42; resolution of, 33, 42–43; and sexual desire, 29–30; theories of, 29–31. See also Child abuse, Single-parent families
Oedipal conflict. See Oedipal behavior
Olson, D. H., 89, 103
Olson, D. R., 1, 4
Oppenheim, D., 91, 104
Other-concept. See Social concept
Overton, W. F., 32, 44

Parental authority, children's perceptions of, 87, 89
Parental omniscience, and Oedipal behavior, 32, 33, 42; assessment of, 36

Parental reporting, 9–10; in assessing Oedipal behavior, 33–34, 39–40
Parent-child relationship, children's perceptions of, 92–94. See also Family relationships
Parke, R. D., 1, 4
Peer relationships: development of, 50; importance of, 6. See also Social support
Perner, J., 86, 104
Perry, T. B., 15, 22, 26
Piaget, J., 48, 52, 65, 85, 86, 87, 98, 104
Pike, R., 14, 26
Pollock, G. H., 29, 44
Portner, J., 89, 103
Projective techiques, 3; limits of, 8. See also Doll play narratives, Separation Anxiety Test

Rabkin, J., 13, 27
Radke-Yarrow, M., 86, 104
Ragozin, A. S., 83
Reid, M., 8, 9, 10, 13, 15, 16, 24, 26, 27
Reznick, J. S., 53, 65
Ridgeway, D., 35, 44, 68, 82, 83, 86, 88, 89, 91, 101, 103, 104
Robertson, J., 49, 65
Robinson, N. M., 83
Roiphe, H., 31, 44
Role intersections, children's understanding of, 30, 32–33, 35, 100–101. See also Family roles
Roopnarine, J. L., 52, 65
Rovine, M., 1, 4
Rygh, J., 86, 104

Sandler, J., 48, 49, 65
Scaife, M., 85–86, 104
Sears, R. R., 29, 44
Seattle Family Behavior Study, 7–8
Self-esteem. See Self-image
Self-image, of children, 1, 6; assessment of, 48–53, 55–56; and emotional support, 24; and Mother-child relationship, 62–64
Self-perception. See Self-image
Self-reliance, and attachment, 77–80
Selman, R. L., 19, 27, 86, 87, 104
Sensitivity, in assessing children's perceptions, 9

Ordering Information

New Directions for Child Development is a series of paperback books that presents the latest research findings on all aspects of children's psychological development, including their cognitive, social, moral, and emotional growth. Books in the series are published quarterly in Fall, Winter, Spring, and Summer and are available for purchase by subscription as well as by single copy.

Subscriptions for 1989-90 cost $48.00 for individuals (a savings of 20 percent over single-copy prices) and $64.00 for institutions, agencies, and libraries. Please do not send institutional checks for personal subscriptions. Standing orders are accepted.

Single copies cost $14.95 when payment accompanies order. (California, New Jersey, New York, and Washington, D.C., residents please include appropriate sales tax.) Billed orders will be charged postage and handling.

Discounts for quantity orders are available. Please write to the address below for information.

All orders must include either the name of an individual or an official purchase order number. Please submit your order as follows:
   Subscriptions: specify series and year subscription is to begin
   Single copies: include individual title code (such as CD1)

Mail all orders to:
   Jossey-Bass Inc., Publishers
   350 Sansome Street
   San Francisco, California 94104

OTHER TITLES AVAILABLE IN THE
NEW DIRECTIONS FOR CHILD DEVELOPMENT SERIES
William Damon, Editor-in-Chief